FEEL GOOD

How to Change Your Mood and Cope with Whatever Comes Your Way

Shane Pascoe and Graham Law

CAPSTONE
A Wiley Brand

Registered office
John Wiley and Sons Ltd, The Atrium, Southern Gate, Chichester, West Sussex, PO19 8SQ, United Kingdom

For details of our global editorial offices, for customer services and for information about how to apply for permission to reuse the copyright material in this book please see our website at www.wiley.com.

Library of Congress Cataloging-in-Publication Data
Pascoe, Shane W.
   Feel good : how to change your mood and cope with whatever comes your way / Shane Pascoe and Graham Law.
      pages cm
   Includes bibliographical references and index.
   ISBN 978-0-857-08452-1 (pbk.)
   1. Mood (Psychology)   2. Emotions.   3. Affect (Psychology)   I. Law, Graham R. II. Title.
   BF521.P37 2014
   152.4—dc23   2013034151

A catalogue record for this book is available from the British Library.

ISBN 978-0-857-08452-1 (paperback)   ISBN 978-0-857-08449-1 (ebk)
ISBN 978-0-857-08451-4 (ebk)

Cover design: Simon Dovar

Set in 11/14 pt Myriad Pro by Toppan Best-set Premedia Limited, Hong Kong
Printed in Great Britain by TJ International Ltd, Padstow, Cornwall, UK

"This fascinating book is a fresh and optimistic guide, offering a balanced insight into taking control of our mood and managing our emotions so we can become healthier and happier, and have a more positive effect on those around us. Seamlessly merging science, philosophy, psychology and spirituality into an accessible and empowering book! A must-read for professionals or students alike."

Hayley Del Sanderson, Principal and Founder, The Yoga Academy

"This is a very welcome book and will appeal to a wide readership and at many levels. It addresses the emotions and feelings that we all experience in life to a greater or lesser degree; and combines sound evidence and therapeutic advice about how to cope and move forward. The approach taken by Graham and Shane is extremely helpful, practical and easy to read; the authors lead readers carefully and explicitly through each chapter. It is highly recommended as a reassuring self-help book and an adjunct book for therapists to use with clients."

Dr Jane Cronin-Davis, Chair of College of Occupational Therapist Specialist Section for Mental Health, guideline development group member for UK National Institute of Clinical Excellence (NICE)

"Explains the concepts and techniques needed by anyone to improve their mood and makes them accessible for everyone to use in everyday situations."

Professor Ian Olver AM, Chief Executive Officer, Cancer Council Australia

"*Feel Good* is a very practical guide to dealing with your mood in daily life. It is easy to read while being based on some of the best current evidence in psychological research."

Professor Mark Harris, UNSW Scientia Professor and Executive Director Centre, Primary Health Care and Equity; and Director, COMPaRE-PHC (Cen... ...agement and Prevention Rese...

To our children, Bethan, Gabi, Kai, and Sophie. Listed in alphabetical order, not a reflection of which ones are our favourites.

CONTENTS

FOREWORD

Many of us suffer short lived fluctuations in mood. These may become entrenched and start to affect the way we live, our personal relationships and our work. Sometimes they may become more severe and need medical or psychological care. Depression and anxiety are common and increasing problems worldwide affecting hundreds of millions of people. So taking action early to break the cycle of negative mood is important. However many mood problems go unrecognized.

Feel Good by Shane Pascoe and Graham Law is a very practical guide to dealing with one's own mood in daily life. The chapters are organized around moods and emotions explaining these and then providing examples of how they be managed. The book describes a number of coping mechanisms and strategies for improving the quality of one's mood. It draws on psychological evidenced-based psychological interventions such as cognitive behavioural therapy and mindfulness.

However the book is not a medical or psychological text and is, of course, not intended to replace professional help. It uses lay language and is easy to read and apply to daily life. As such it fills an important gap and will help boost your "mental health literacy" – the essential knowledge and skill that we all need to stay healthy and function better in our lives.

Mark Harris
Scientia Professor and Director of the Centre for Primary Health Care and Equity, University of South Wales

PREFACE

In the Arizona desert there is a physical representation of what we have tried to do with this book. Frank Lloyd Wright built a home, a workplace, a school and so much more in Taliesin West. His motivation was to deal with the ideas the landscape inspired in him, and what he achieved was the bringing together of all the best elements from all of his achievements. All the best elements of helping people over the years have been brought together here. The people Shane has seen have often had significant trauma and prolonged distress. The lessons learnt in helping these people are the same we have distilled here, to help people who may have experienced something similar if not necessarily as intense. Graham has considerable experience in the science of health and disease research. On a personal level he has tried to improve physically, mentally and emotionally. This journey, with the invaluable support of his wife and children, led through mindfulness and yoga to a calm and fulfilling life.

Writing together has enabled us to bridge the disciplines we have found fascinating over the years: education, psychology, philosophy and medicine. It is through these experiences we have been privileged to sit with the patients and students who have inspired us, lucky enough to see the brilliance of other professionals we have worked with and generally kept going to address the needs of those that come through the door every day.

ACKNOWLEDGEMENTS

Asiyah for knowing when to smile and urge Shane on and when to smile and point out the magic beans that lie in his hand. Nicki for her unstinting inspiration and ability to finish things. Shiraz Rehman for his amazing assistance in negotiating contracts and asking all the right questions, all the time. Morris Averill for looking at every angle and beyond to get the best out of this project for everyone. Ben Treverton for his great photography.

To the team at Capstone; Iain Campbell, Holly Bennion, Jonathan Shipley, Jenny Ng, Vicky Kinsman, Megan Saker, Emily Bryczkowski, Samantha Hartley and Louise Campbell.

To the friends who looked over the draft; Jeremy Miles, Natasha Grabham, Geraldine Carroll, Christina Bossinakis, Dom Hilbrink, Ben Treverton, Tim Manning, Bibiana Chan, Fiona Skewes, Nick Campbell, Rachel Madden, Mark Harris, Ian Olver and Angelo Kapsalis.

Illustration credits:
Hot Air Balloons, Detailed Vector Collection – PILart/Shutterstock.com.
Sheet of paper for notes and paperclip – Sergign/Shutterstock.com.

ABOUT THE AUTHORS

Dr Shane Pascoe

Shane Pascoe is a husband, father, and a danger to himself and others with a tool in his hand. Since graduating from the University of Newcastle, Shane has worked in the field of Psychology in a variety of different roles in several countries. He has practised meditation since being introduced to it by a group of cancer patients.

Dr Graham Law

Graham Law is a senior lecturer at the Leeds School of Medicine in England. He is a scientist in health research and leads a team looking at the impact of sleep on our metabolism and general health. He has published over 75 papers in peer-reviewed journals, and this is his second book published with Shane. Graham is a keen practitioner of yoga and mindfulness. His wife and two children are the core of his life and provide continuous meaning and support.

Chapter 1

"HOW ARE YOU?"

When someone asks "How are you?" it can set off a cascade of thoughts in your mind. Despite the fact that this has become a greeting, it is a serious question and it makes you wonder "What mood am I in?" Have you ever examined your mood and what impact it has on your life? This book will help you to explore a range of mood issues that confront people every day, addressing the characteristic feelings and emotions, the triggers and outcomes. Of course, you are also reading this to discover what you can do about these issues. This book will show you strategies that can be used to overcome mood problems and lead a happier and more content life.

The chapters in this book are organized around the moods and emotions that people feel, both positive and negative, all of the time. Your mood is your conscious state of mind or your predominant emotion. Mood is an umbrella term for all the emotions and affective states that you experience. An emotion is a more specific term than mood. An emotion is your perception of a feeling, more related to individual experiences. The affective state is a technical term, from psychology, and relates to what is seen on the outside as a sum of all those moods and feelings you subjectively experience. Moods have what is known as a "valence", which describes overall whether the mood you are experiencing is either positive or negative. The valence of a mood has become part of our everyday language; it is commonplace for someone to describe themselves as being in a good mood, or a bad mood, or their mood is low.

This book deals with issues around moods such as hope, anger, distress, unhappiness, well-being and self-esteem. All of us must deal with these moods during our lives. An important starting point is for you to identify which of these mood issues you are experiencing and the extent to which they are operating. Chapter 2 will help you to think about the ways moods develop and how these may influence your life. Chapters 3 to 8 cover some of the different moods you may experience, both positive and negative, in more detail and within each of these chapters there are coping mechanisms and strategies for improving the quality of your mood. The final three chapters cover more general techniques to improve your mood and your ability to cope whatever comes your way.

Why do I experience moods?

It does seem odd to me, when we are a technologically advanced society, and humans have become powerful over nature, able to cure disease, start wars, fly to the moon, and yet, you and I still experience the feelings of emotion which contribute to something so primeval as a mood. Scientists have identified that emotions developed in animals to help us survive in our environment. Emotions are experienced by lots of different animals – as you could imagine when you see a cat running away from a perceived threat, the cat is more than likely scared. When a dog is barking we assume it is angry. An emotional response has been an essential part of the survival of our species, and we accept and embrace many emotions such as happiness and affection.

However, a problem is encountered when your mood, or its valence, has a detrimental effect on your life. Some philosophers, such as Plato, believed that emotions were undesirable and sometimes evil. This view does not exist now, and we understand that emotions are essential and often a very positive source of motivation. You will be taken through a range of the moods describing positive and negative aspects and sometimes the underlying physiology that will help to explain your feelings and responses to situations. To be clear, your physiology is the state of your body, the processes which happen that are beyond your active conscious control.

Some clarification about the use of the words positive and negative when talking about emotions. We use the terms positive and negative as they are widely understood and help us group the kinds of emotions that people generally want to experience more of (positive emotions such as joy) and those they want to manage better or reduce (negative emotions such as anger and frustration). Negative emotions such as anger can have a useful outcome in that when angry we are more likely to stand up for our rights – providing a drive to be assertive as opposed to passive in a situation where our rights are violated.

A bit about us

My name is Shane, and I live and work in Newcastle in Australia. I have extensive experience working as a psychologist, in the community and in hospital settings, and as a scientist. I will be drawing on these experiences throughout this book. In my work I have met many people dealing with all sorts of issues, from the very severe and serious mental health problems through to more minor mood issues that cause them problems. In my scientific work as a health researcher and whilst gaining my PhD, I have collaborated with Dr Graham Law, who is a medical scientist and statistician.

Graham lives in York in England and is Head of Biostatistics for an Institute within the School of Medicine at Leeds University. He has published over 75 scientific research papers, and two books, and leads fellow scientists within an academic environment. His knowledge and experience will help in interpreting the scientific findings so that you can be reassured that there is good evidence for you to base your decisions on.

I will take the things that work best when people struggle with their mood, to give you hope and optimism in dealing with your own issues. I aim to prevent the downward spiral that is character-istic of mood disorders. By using these stories I hope that the knowledge that patients, psychologists and scientists have acquired through their journey can be helpful to you.

When I see people as a psychologist my opening question is usually "How are you?" This is a simple start, and yet this straight-forward question can bring forward a wave of thoughts, memories and feelings into the open and make them accessible to analysis. The main issues we talk about, often for hours, are their thoughts. Each person brings with them an amazing story. If I were speaking with you, my hope would be to understand how you got to where you are, how you arrived there in the first place and why you keep returning to the same place. My objective is for you to feel better. During our sessions together, people usually thank me for under-standing where they are coming from and pointing them in the right direction to show them a way to feeling better. I hold their hand. That is all, a guiding hand.

Why do you need this book?

All of us have moods that go up and down: that is completely normal. It is also reasonable to assume that any mood you are experiencing will not last forever. This includes both good and bad moods, and often time is one of the most important parts of dealing with a distressing mood.

This book, and the techniques we will show you, will help you to work out why you feel the way you do. It will help you to discover the reasons behind some of your thoughts and the reason you are experiencing a feeling. It will also describe, and walk you through, some effective techniques to help you deal with these mood issues. If, however, your mood is impacting in a serious way on your life, you should seek professional advice. This book is not a replacement for medical and psychological care when that is necessary.

Fundamental principles

I will be using some of the key principles that I use in my work; they will help you to explore your feelings, look at the consequences of your mood, and hopefully develop some strategies to feel good. The fundamental principles that I start with are listed in the box below. Knowledge, or content, is what you say or the actual verbatim words you use. It is overt and extrinsic. But of course, this is often less interesting than what is going on underneath, the subtext or other meaning you can establish from delivering the words.

Principles of therapy

- The attitudes and concepts are more important than the knowledge.
- An empathic response is the only way forward – for others and indeed yourself.
- All behaviour has a function.
- Collaboration is the way.
- Remember content and process.

As an example you may say "I really like going to work". The words are the "content" of the message. "Process" is everything else: tone, syntax and semantics, and conveys a meaning intrinsically. The statement above could be phrased as a question if there is a rising tone at the end of the sentence, or as a statement of fact. The process or way you speak the statement guides the listener to the next step, and if phrased as a question leads you to attempt to answer the question. If you fail to show enthusiasm when conveying your exclamation about going to work, or you often come in late or call in sick for work, then the process says a lot more than the content. So is the statement "I really like going to work" correct? You can use the understanding of process to develop insight into the situation, and to respond accordingly.

The hardest parts to therapy are being attentive to the feelings of the client: listening. In this book you will learn the skills of listening to yourself, gaining insight in a way that involves warmth and genuineness. There are reasons you do what you do or as many therapists say "Behaviour is functional". When I sit with a person in therapy they often present a list of symptoms, sometimes in a letter from their doctor. These allow me to give you a direction and we talk about what these symptoms mean to you. This collaboration is the way therapy works, and this book will allow a similar collaborative effort to develop.

How you can use this book

The content of the book is important but it is not the main aspect of what we hope you will achieve by reading it. To get the most out of this experience, we suggest reading a chapter per week to allow enough time to play with some of the concepts you have read. Allow yourself the time to think about the relevance each chapter has to you, explore the concepts and engage in the techniques introduced throughout.

With help from Graham, I will detail the latest research and you will use evidence-based strategies to make the changes required using a simple "post-it" note technique. You will also find helpful boxes throughout, marked with a hot-air balloon icon, which offer insightful scientific material which supports the techniques and learning you will develop along the way.

Some might say that this represents being filled with hot air, but I like to think it is a symbol that is going places, exactly as I hope you will be during this book. A lesson in metaphor I guess.

Using the "post-it" note technique

My first supervisor had a powerful intellect. He always made progress with the most difficult problems, and with the hardest cases, by moving with his clients to a point of hope. Where there was light at the end of the tunnel. He did this by condensing all his knowledge on a discipline and a subject to a simple "post-it" note. We will use "post-it" notes in this book to remind you of what techniques to practise.

The "post-it" note strips away any pretence at being too intellectual or clever in addressing very complex problems you face. People have a short attention span and often this is out of necessity. Your world may be traumatic and requires you to look everywhere for threats, seemingly at the same time. By being concise, the unnecessary aspects to theory and any hyperbole are removed, leaving the honest and open discussion about your problem at hand. Once you master the skill, you can move on. Now let's get started with our first "post-it" note technique on the next page.

Each chapter covers a different type of mood

At this point, a descriptive list of feelings and emotions would seem a simple way for you to map your mood to the chapters.

"Post-it" note technique

On a "post-it" note, write down a few words or sentences on why you bought this book, or why you picked it off the shelf. Or perhaps someone else bought this book for you; what do you think they wanted you to explore? You could write down your most important goals. What do you hope to achieve by reading this book?

Take some time over this, give it some thought. You may wish to improve your overall mood, or there may be parts of your life that you wish to be improved. For example, I would write down that I want to strike a better balance between my work and family life. But what you write will be personal to you. This exercise may feel uncomfortable, but please persevere.

Now put the note somewhere safe. You might leave it in this book, or stick it up in a room in your house. As the weeks go by and you become more self-aware, you may want to add to this note, or change it.

Unfortunately this is oversimplifying a complex series of issues and you won't benefit from this book using that approach. I must ask you to indulge me by spending time reading each chapter to gain maximum benefit.

Chapter 2 focuses on your hopes for your future, by looking at how questioning your beliefs and thoughts can help you achieve your goal to feel good. It will help you to assess how sound your thoughts are which is the basis of the theories we use.

Anger is a normal emotion for humans, as it is an essential skill used for survival. Anger becomes a problem when it is not managed properly and Chapter 3 deals with this issue.

Chapter 4 discusses some of the strengths you have, and your belief in your capabilities, which is referred to as self-efficacy. Strengthening your self-efficacy will lead to improvements in your achievements, and allow you to improve your mood.

Chapter 5 explores distress and ways to deal with it. The word distress is sometimes used interchangeably with the word stress. However as you will discover this is not strictly correct. A life with no stress is impossible but you will learn how to avoid it impacting negatively on you and therefore causing distress.

The identification and strategies for dealing with low mood, or depression as it is sometimes called, are in Chapter 6 "Unhappiness". Depression is the sadness a person experiences when they think about earlier life experiences or their future. It is a lethargy that permeates the soul of the person and marks their thinking. This chapter will outline how depression influences a person's thinking in the most negative of ways.

Your feeling of well-being, explored in Chapter 7, tries to bring out in you positive ways to improve your feelings about your achievements and where you are. Chapter 8 will help you to examine your self-esteem, and to develop ways to improve this mood. These two features of your mood have been repeatedly connected with good health and quality of life.

Chapters 9 and 10 are designed to consolidate the techniques you have been developing and to introduce some methods to improve your mood and well-being. These involve techniques such as mindfulness, sleep hygiene and relaxation methods. And rounding this all off in Chapter 11 I will ask you to see how far you have come. You will realize the distance travelled over the course of working through the book.

Myths around mood are harmful

Why am I introducing myths at this point? Some myths are traditions, accepted ways of doing things that are often unquestioned. Many of these myths, at their core, are mistaken beliefs that are shown to be false through evidence.

A common myth around mood issues is believing a person should "get on with it", show a "stiff upper lip", or "pull their socks up". Through self-improvement, accessing treatment where required, gaining support from friends and family and just living their life, many people are showing a level of achievement which is commendable and should not be minimized. Some people think that having mood problems is equivalent to having a weak mind. I wonder if those same people would have the courage to continue holding onto that myth of a weak mind after a discussion with Churchill who suffered from his own problems with low mood.

More extreme myths lead to people with more serious issues being painted as violent, or incompetent. These simplistic notions end up making people feel objectified, not a person anymore but a scary monster to be feared or ridiculed. It affects a person's view of themselves, and when a person accepts these prejudiced views, people who need real help are reluctant to seek treatment, or withdraw from life. The person's self-worth suffers. Attitudes such as these usually involve inaccurate information, with the outcomes being hurtful depictions in the media or as the subject of jokes.

Starting to deal with mood issues begins with respect for yourself

How you acquire self-respect can be as simple as using respectful language both when talking about others but especially about yourself. Things such as "a person who has diabetes" is more respectful than labelling a person "diabetic". Of course this is not about the issues around controlling your glucose, but it is important that society, and you, recognize that labels can lead to problems. By emphasizing abilities, you highlight strength, identify opportunities and are not constrained by the language of limitation.

When you do not respect yourself, this can lead to many difficulties, which some people describe as the "sick role". Talcott Parsons described this first, in 1951, where being "sick" was perceived as having benefits for the person, giving an individual a reason for not completing their various responsibilities. It is easy to take on this attitude when there is no visible injury, but the person reports a low mood. If you think in terms of people looking to benefit from some low mood, or the sick role, then it is a slippery slope ending in labels such as "waster" or "slack" to describe people that do not seem to be able to operate at their full capability.

A common belief is that "if I can't see it then it doesn't exist". Although your mind does not have a cast on it like a broken leg would, when a person suffers a mood issue, they need the same kind of support a pair of crutches can bring. For the mind to really heal, it requires weeks if not months of care and attention to learn and implement the strategies required to manage your mood.

Cognitive Behavioural Therapy may help

You might have heard the phrase "you think the way you feel". Your thoughts and beliefs determine your emotions and, in many cases, your behaviours. In Cognitive Behavioural Therapy (CBT) this can be explained with the ABC model. An activating event (A) initiates a belief (B) and a belief causes an emotion or other consequence (C). Therefore, your thoughts and beliefs determine your emotions and, in many cases, your behaviours. This is a difficult concept to understand, let alone apply. It is a process that takes time whilst simultaneously dealing with distress. It has been compared to juggling a whole lot of burning torches and I say "in order for you to extinguish the torches and stop juggling, you first must read a book on how to juggle and extinguish torches, all the while you are still juggling."

CBT looks at the strategies and mechanisms of change. One way it does this is by looking at the causes of behaviours and describing the change processes themselves. This could help you to handle the process of change and to engage in effective behaviour to feel good. CBT also hopes to improve motivation to reach goals. While doing this, it aims to decrease the thoughts and emotions that interfere with helpful behaviours. Through this process you increase your distress tolerance and hopefully you move more of your helpful behaviours from just intentions, to the broader world and your life.

CBT uses interventions such as getting you to measure your thoughts, feelings and behaviours. It uses problem solving and exposure strategies to change the process and reactions you have. One of the major aspects to CBT is cognitive modification or changing your thoughts.

A different way of thinking

CBT is a change technology, but there are many disadvantages and traps to applying this technology. The traps are that I must avoid arguing with you about the beliefs you hold dear. As detailed above, these beliefs are encased in a fortress of past experiences, many of them distressing, a fear of the future and a belief that there is nothing worth doing anyway. When someone says they are bad and do not deserve good things, it is very hard for me to not reinforce that being judgemental saying "no, you are a good person."

These change processes identify thinking that is unhelpful. To challenge the use of these thoughts does not motivate you to change by itself and does not, on its own, resolve issues with mood. To change your mood takes time. It often involves using a thought to deal with a feeling. In this book we offer a simpler and easier way to manage your mood.

It will introduce methods that have been proposed from argumentative theory. This is based on the fact that humans are not good at using reasoning alone to make decisions. Such decisions will be based on bias and produce a poor outcome and we will explore the ways you should examine your decisions, and how these impact on your mood.

Moods impact on well-being and health

What are the consequences of poor mood management? Why should you be concerned with your anger, or your anxiety? A person may think and believe that the world is a dark place, filled with disappointment or, in the case of anxiety, danger at every turn. The world itself has too many obstacles and too few positive aspects to sustain them. If this person is asked about their future, again the hopeless feelings emerge and a perceived lack of problem-solving and "people skills" are added to the list of crimes this person believes they are guilty of. This leads to further isolation and avoidance.

The consequences differ between the various mood issues you may have, but when people manage their moods poorly there are serious impacts for the individual, their friends and family, and society as a whole. Negative moods can lead to rumination, where you are obsessed with physical symptoms of your mood, rather than the cause. A person might have serious problems with depression, anxiety or anger.

A particularly difficult consequence of a negative mood can be the problems a person may face in making decisions and using their judgement. This can lead to further anxiety about the "wrong" decision being made and increase the downward spiral. Others may be dealing with social relationships in a negative or even destructive way. A person with low mood may be using, unconsciously, strategies to evoke support and feedback from their loved ones. Or, in others, the opposite strategy of closing themselves off may be used. This can create distance and frustrations in people who may be part of their support network.

This book aims to empower you

The main aim of this book is the delivery of content. However, the exercises you do, the thoughts you have and write on the "post-it" notes are often where you will learn most about yourself, your interpersonal relationships and how you change over time.

As you read through this book, you might well think "this isn't rocket science you know". I take this as a compliment. To me it is a job well done, apart from the way your own mood is now better managed, it means the insight and understanding you have will better serve you when you are challenged again or when you hear a friend experiencing similar problems.

Either way, we hope that by the end of the book, you will feel able to implement the changes you wish to make and also take the next step on your journey; whether like mine it involved writing a book or fulfilling some grand dream of your own. You may need to take a chance to benefit from the risks you have gambled on, and this may be the start of your personal journey. You may need to show courage in placing yourself in a vulnerable position, but

"Post-it" note technique

In therapy, outrageous as this may seem, it is possible to use a single session to make significant progress. It cannot be used with very serious issues, and there are benefits for everyone to spend time contemplating an issue. But, a solution-focused single session therapy assumes that there is one session to make change: one shot.

This method can help you begin developing your strategies for change. I know you haven't yet explored your issues, I will do that later, but I would like you to consider how confident you are that you will be able to attain your goal or goals whatever they may be.

On the "post-it" note from the first technique above, write your confidence in attaining your objective out of ten for each goal, with zero being not at all confident and ten being as confident as you can be. Don't worry if your confidence is low. The aim is to improve your confidence as you work through this book.

in doing this you are able to draw on your wealth of experience that will see you overcome amazing odds.

You are now ready to proceed. Take your time with each chapter, and aim to spend at least a week on each chapter to allow the material to sink in and for you to give it some consideration.

Chapter 2

CHALLENGE
YOUR
THINKING

It is only after confronting difficulties that we know how strong we really are. In talking with a 36-year-old statistician, he described how he would look back on his problems and our attempts at learning from them, noting "I would write down the pearls of wisdom. I began testing my requirement for worry. Right now doesn't explain what happened five years ago or what will happen five years from now." This is how you can challenge your negative thoughts and test them out. What is the evidence for and against? How realistic are they? This is called problem-solving thinking.

This chapter will discuss how your thinking affects your mood and how challenging these thoughts can help in managing mood problems, by covering many aspects of science and psychology. The ideas and processes here, including discussion on beliefs, optimism, bias and motivation, will greatly enhance your ability to work through your issues and to help yourself feel good. By the end of this chapter you will have explored the thoughts you have, and be able to recognize any bias, making progress through greater understanding. This will build your optimism and confidence, providing hope and putting you in a better place to change your thinking.

In his book *Incognito* (2011) David Eagleman described thoughts as being underpinned by physical things. He identified that thoughts and feelings are often not under your control. What does this mean in practice? An illustration can be seen in the range of thoughts the same event can trigger in different people. A happy person may think a ringing telephone signals a good friend wanting a chat. An anxious person however hearing the same phone may be thinking that bad news is about to be delivered. The choices are made as the result of programmes in the brain, which operate like a computer. Eagleman also identified that consciousness is often not involved. The conscious mind is like an abridged version of what is happening behind the scenes: your conscious thoughts are only a small portion of all of the mental processing going on.

The unconscious mind can identify danger long before the conscious mind is aware. Graham explains a novel experiment that shows how good the unconscious mind can be in the box below. I will explore this ability further but let's look at those thoughts and processes you have as part of your conscious awareness.

Good decks and bad decks

Bechara and colleagues published a study in 1997, where participants were presented with four decks, or packs, of cards and were asked to pick cards from any deck. Each card had either a financial reward or penalty on it. The cards from the "good decks" had an overall financial reward whilst those from "bad decks" had a financial penalty overall. Participants were given money with each card they picked. People started by choosing cards from all decks but after about 40–50 cards had worked out which were the "good decks".

The unconscious mind worked it out first; a stress response was detected when the participant selected a card from the "bad decks" after selecting only 10 cards. The physical measures were present when picking the high risk cards before the person could get a hunch or develop a concept as to what was going on.

Your beliefs will affect your mood

What is responsible for changing your mood? As mentioned in Chapter 1 "How are you?" there are many factors that contribute to your mood, some good and some bad. The genetics that you are born with, biochemical changes in your body and your life experiences can all have an effect on your mood. Which one thing can you put your finger on and say with certainty this is "why" you are feeling how you do? At present, science cannot give us that answer but often we act as if we are certain and make decisions based on this certainty. And many times these decisions turn out to be incorrect.

When you have a fixed belief in something your behaviour should be consistent with that belief. For example, it is commonplace for people to read newspapers that will support their own belief systems: a person with right-wing or conservative political tendencies will prefer to read a paper that supports those tendencies and vice versa. When the ideas that you come across are in conflict with that belief, you will experience what is known as cognitive dissonance and this is problematic to our fundamental desire for harmony. Cognitive dissonance induces uncomfortable feelings and to resolve this dissonance you could change your belief and harmony is restored.

Someone trying to help, by speaking to a person who is troubled may slip into a similar trap. This is when a therapist or helper contradicts a person, inducing cognitive dissonance in the person they are trying to help. For example, I may be speaking with someone who is feeling unhappy with their life and they tell me that they are feeling worthless; they believe this is the case, with certainty. As a caring human it is tempting for me to jump in and give the person concrete evidence that this is not the case: highlighting all the good they have done or the roles they have fulfilled as a friend, family member or colleague. This results in cognitive dissonance as they begin to feel that even a therapist doesn't believe them. As a therapist I work hard to avoid this.

You may notice well-meaning friends or family using this tactic. They feel that they are helping, but it may have a negative effect. I will try very hard not to do this in this book. An aphorism that may apply here is "The road to hell is paved with good intentions" and we as helpers should avoid that trap.

How to start the search for "why"

One of the questions that you may want to ask is "why?" Why am I feeling this way, either positive or negative? Science has some trouble with the "why" question and this is due to the way science is defined. It is a common misconception that science provides all of the answers in all fields of human endeavour. Graham explains why this is not the case in the box which follows as he discusses the scientific method and how this leads to such a commonplace misconception.

Scientific method and why

When science investigates why something happened, then fundamentally it engages the scientific method which has been used successfully for many centuries. It assumes that it is not possible to know the "truth". This is where belief systems diverge from empirically-based or scientific approaches. A belief system, such as a religion, provides what it considers to be true about humans and life. This does not require evidence, but requires faith for the believer. In contrast, a scientist develops an explanation for things he or she observes and this is called a hypothesis.

(Continued)

But even using the objective measurement of things that science employs introduces a paradox: science is performed by humans and therefore involves thoughts which are subjective and irrational at times. Koestler, in 1971, writes succinctly that evidence can confirm the predictions made by a theory but it can't confirm the theory itself. In other words it cannot very easily answer the question about why.

Koestler provided a good historical example where Babylonian astronomers made precise predictions that worked, as they were able to calculate the length of a year close to 0.001 per cent of the value we now think is correct. But when the Babylonians asked why the day was this given length, they chose an explanation where the planets were Gods and their movement defined the health and well-being of both men and the states they lived in. Another example comes from Christopher Columbus, who is credited with initiating European contact with the Americas in the 15th and 16th centuries, was able to sail by the stars but couldn't tell you what gravity was or whether the planets moved in elliptical orbits or not. This is an example of humans only being able to confirm a prediction, the length of the year, as opposed to explaining why this happened.

The problem with the explanations for the "why" in these instances is that you may think you know the reasons. Each reason is supported in your mind by your perceived ability to predict, but you may be way off the mark. A good scientist will tell you that there are some things that they are happy they understand and feel confident they have identified the why. But still they will say that none of these are known with certainty. Therefore even when you think you know something, you need to constantly check your theories and assumptions against the available evidence.

One of the explanations that you may use is described by the tendency people have to blame someone's personality for their behaviour, rather than the situation they find themselves in. This is known as a personality-based explanation. The identification of this tendency was supported in a study by Jones and Harris (1967) that required people to read essays that were either for or against Fidel Castro, a polarizing figure in the United States of America at the time. The participants were then asked to rate the attitudes of the writers towards Fidel Castro.

The participants tended to attribute cause to the person, not the situation. When study participants believed that the writers freely chose what to write, they rated the authors of pro-Castro essays as having a more positive attitude towards him than those who wrote anti-Castro essays. When people were told that the writer's opinion, for or against Castro in essays, was assigned randomly, they still rated writers who spoke in support of Castro as having a more positive attitude towards him compared to those who spoke against him. The situation that the writers were in, either naturally or assigned, was not taken into account by the participants in the study reading the essays. They attributed this attitude to the writers' disposition instead. The objective and logical aspects to explain why people wrote the essays they did were ignored in the opinions the readers formed.

Rest assured, this tendency to make assumptions, to not consider evidence fully, is not just something you do. Rather worryingly, there are many aspects to what people do in healthcare, medicine and surgery that just plain don't work. There are problems with the quality of care provided, decision making, biases both within and outside of the systems used and problems with the science.

This was recognized by Archie Cochrane, a Scottish physician in the 20th century, who noted that only some interventions offered in medicine actually worked. He was instrumental in developing "evidence-based medicine", which uses science and expert opinion to inform healthcare about the approaches that are beneficial, and as importantly which ones do harm. Evidence-based medicine is "the conscientious, explicit, and judicious use of current best evidence in making decisions about the care of individual patients . . . from systematic research" (Sackett et al., 1996).

When the health professional is an evidence-based practitioner they must decide which, of the huge amount of published research, is the best evidence. The Cochrane Collaboration is a global not-for-profit organization that facilitates development of approaches to healthcare, using a standardized approach to finding evidence and choosing how it feeds into practice (see http://www.cochrane.org/). You need to do a similar thing when examining which of your beliefs and thoughts are beneficial and which ones are causing you harm. Let's now look at how you can do this. By analyzing the biases and unhelpful thinking styles associated with moods you are able to manage them better.

Optimism will bring hope for your future

In improving mood, I teach optimism as a skill which fosters hope that you will be able to make things change and improve. Optimism, originally derived from the word optimum which means best, is where present conditions and future events are viewed as being optimal, the best they can be. To summarize the work of Scioli and colleagues, optimists are those that expect things to go their way, but this thought must be grounded squarely in reason. There is evidence to support optimism as a belief that you actually can do something about the problem you are facing. This will be covered in more detail in Chapter 4 "Self-efficacy".

The opposite of such optimism, where you identify negative views of yourself, the world and your future is one thing that may seem straightforward to identify or change. However, having to live with these concerns constantly may be far worse than you imagine. The absolute tyranny of these beliefs and thoughts, constant and unchanging, can be difficult to bear. These can often be phrased as "I could, but" type statements, where any other view is seen as not possible, or not likely to lead to a good outcome. The person is, in many ways, attached to their beliefs. To help break this, they can experiment with that same attachment and find out whether it indeed works or not.

Reasoning has benefits for clear thinking

Reasoning is the process by which you think, understand and form judgements using logic. The reasoned elements of argument are therefore linked by logic. The principles of logical argument are described by Graham in the box on the following page – it has a long tradition, and is still used in science and mathematics.

We must, however, be specific here as subjective feelings or value judgements cannot be challenged by logical argument. The basis of a logical argument means there can be no other solution, and if there is, our job in debating is to see where one or indeed both arguments might contain an error. Then we can resolve the error and continue our search for the correct answer.

The discussions I have with people are coated in language around mood, knowledge of their condition, coping skills, and how they modulate these issues. I talk about their physical, emotional and mental development, their current life situation, their motivation and expectations. I do this to develop reasoning.

Principles of logic

A logical argument starts with one or more premises. These premises may be facts, or assumed to be facts, that can be used to justify the truth of an argument or can support a conclusion from an argument. To these premises, a principle of logic is applied in order to come to a conclusion. Logic is used to find consistency or inconsistency in predictions from the premises we have. But the principles can be used by you to explore things you think about. A simple example is:

Premise: John is in my class
Premise: All of my class passed their exams
Logical conclusion: John passed his exams

The conclusion, using logic, seems sensible. Despite the logic being sound, we are relying on the truth and accuracy of the premises. This conclusion is the same when repeated, whether it is completed by me or by you and indeed at any time. You have a sound argument when the logic is valid, the premises are true, and therefore you can trust that the conclusion must also be true. Any deviation from this, for example one premise not being true, results in a conclusion that is also not true.

Let me explain. Mercier, who is a research scientist, developed a theory that looked at just these things and which was published in 2011; he called this "argumentative theory". He pointed out that reason allows the mind to go beyond perception, habit and instinct. Just like a child, you make mental models of the world outside, within the confines of your imagination and in many ways you play with these models. You imagine all the different scenarios that are possible, coming up with scenes and playing out the scripts within your own head. When you do this over long periods of time, you develop habits and reason allows you to consider other alternatives to the well-worn paths of previous experience.

This ability to explore possible outcomes in our minds is what sets us apart from nearly all other animals. Reason also allows you to question your "gut reactions" and see if it is safe to consider alternate ideas. This provides an introduction to new experiences in a safe way because you think about them first.

There are many pieces of evidence, however, that don't support the use of reasoning in making decisions. In spite of this people use reason anyway. This happens in some cases more than others. When people know their decisions are to be publicized, or when they are giving advice, they rely more on reason.

Your conclusions should rely on evidence

There must be a relationship between the conclusion you draw and the reasons for accepting it. As a useful analogy given by Mercier, imagine that there is an actor and you are the audience; the actor aims to convince you to change your thoughts and you are unconvinced but willing to change if given the right reasons. Let's examine this further in terms of outcomes. Many people aim for a positive outcome, and this may involve indulging yourself in something pleasurable. You feel you need a reason for indulgence even though it doesn't change the quality of the experience. You expect more negative and fewer positive feelings when you indulge without a reason, compared to when you indulge with a reason. When people give themselves an indulgence as a way of soothing a poor performance as opposed to rewarding good performance, the same is true. People expect positive feelings to happen. However your actual experience diverges from the expectation. You love a chocolate just as much whether you had a reason to enjoy it or not. An association between justification and indulgence is not required for you to have a good experience although your reasoning and beliefs may tell you otherwise.

Research by Erika Okada (2005) has shown that we are willing to spend more time on our hedonistic goals than those which are most useful. Reviewing this work, you see that when hedonistic and utilitarian options are presented together, you can trust your brain to give you a good outcome in terms of what is the greatest good. Hedonism is your way of looking inward for maximum happiness, whilst utilitarianism is looking outwards for maximum happiness in society. However, when presented with a utilitarian choice and then a hedonistic one, the pleasure principle wins out. The way forward is to learn from your experiences not your beliefs and take note of experiences which are inconsistent with beliefs.

Reasoning is also, unfortunately, prone to bias

There are many biases that have been identified with our thinking and we will now go through some common ones. A bias is where something leans to the side; it is not correct. For example, the Leaning Tower of Pisa is biased. It should be vertical but leans to one side. Let's begin with the problems of using logical arguments including what is known as confirmation bias, and things that don't follow known as non-sequiturs. The next box contains a list of some of these commonly-seen biases in thinking.

If you are providing arguments to support your actions, you are more than likely producing confirmation bias. Confirmation bias

Some of the more common biases in thinking

- Confirmation bias
- What you see is what you get
- Non-sequitur
- Ad ignorantiam
- Inappropriate categorization
- Self-serving bias
- Biased-assimilation process

is the tendency to favour information that reinforces your assumptions. Graham will explain further in the next box.

Remember back in school when you were forced to debate with other students? You could come up with a plethora of reasons why something wasn't the case. The good thing about debates is that they make you generate rebuttals and push you to give a detailed explanation, while providing evidence. Whether you agree or disagree, you try and confirm your initial stance. You use reasoning therefore to confirm your opinion.

When you just accept a premise as being factual, such as when something is said by someone in authority, you may have a problem. So the first step is to look at the premises. The second step is to look at your logic. As we have mentioned, the brain is very good at developing rough guides to navigate the world but often these are just that: rough. This has been defined as "What You See Is All There Is" (WYSIATI) by Daniel Kahneman (2011), where the human mind will make an assessment regardless of the quality of the information that the person has available to them.

Confirmation bias

As Shane said, confirmation bias is the tendency for you to favour information that reinforces your assumptions or preconceived ideas. This gives rise to one of the other names that this bias is known by: "myside bias". But how does this come about?

People don't necessarily look for evidence that is counter to an existing belief. People in general ignore negative arguments and they are not very good at generating or anticipating counter arguments or even generating rebuttals. This results in a biased search for information. They tend to either group together facts that shouldn't go together or make exceptions from an argument that they disagree with. They especially do this when the subject we are thinking about is emotionally charged. Even after finding the evidence and interpreting it, possibly in a neutral manner, a person still retains the ability to memorize the information in a biased way. All in all we are not good at objective assessment of information that we have a prior interest in. As Francis Bacon in 1620 said:

> For a man always believes more readily that which he prefers.

This has been a key method for survival. However, our world has changed now. We can't necessarily accept that what we see is all there is. This rough guide only hampers us in applying logic.

Everybody loves stories, and when you can weave a story into a series of facts this gives you an impression of greater understanding. However, this may be flawed or biased, and the facts should not be weaved together. We have limited ability to resist this though. When someone jumps ahead of you in a queue at the shops, you may invent a story that they did that on purpose because they think you won't argue with them. Or they did that because they are late for something important. Neither of these stories may be true, but you still invent them.

There are a host of other biases to avoid

Psychologists and scientists have identified many other biases in thinking. When conclusions don't follow premises we have a problem called a "non-sequitur". This is a Latin phrase meaning "it does not follow" and refers to the error of coming to a conclusion that does not follow the premises on which it is based. An example when thinking about climate change was described in the *Observer* newspaper and gives us a word, "therefore", to look for in our own thinking:

> Warming was caused by sunspots, or fluctuations in the Earth's orbit, or volcanic eruptions. Therefore it cannot be caused by mankind. The "therefore" is the giveaway, the delicious *non sequitur*: just because Earth has warmed for one or another reason in the past is no reason why it cannot warm for a completely different reason in the future. (Llewellyn, 2007)

Other logical errors occur when you support an argument by stating that there is no evidence that it isn't true (ad ignorantiam). Looking more closely at this there is an important distinction to be drawn between evidence of no effect and no evidence of an effect. Many a politician has fallen into this trap. For example, take any number of "health scares" over the past few decades and you will find this to be the case. In using logic, the most important rule is that in order to make a positive claim, positive evidence for that specific claim must be provided. Absence of another explanation only means that you do not know something; it doesn't mean you get to make up an explanation.

When you think in terms of a continuum, errors of logic such as creating categories when there are none or grouping together items when it is difficult to establish categories are both errors of logic. You come across a simple example all of the time. It is common to be asked your age on a form in categories. So when you are 39 years and 364 days you are in the 34–39-year-old category. Age one day and you go up to a considerably older age group.

A similar issue occurs when you accept one position along the scale of a debate but this does not mean you also accept the extreme of the position along that same scale. A good example is your view on discipline for children. You may believe discipline is important, but this does not mean you support somebody hitting their child. The extreme, beating a child, is not the same as gentle discipline for a more extreme misdemeanour.

The "self-serving bias" is an interesting process whereby people generally have a tendency to attribute good or indeed positive outcomes to a personal factor they possess and to attribute bad or negative outcomes to external or other factors that are outside their control. For example: "If I speed and don't get into a crash it's because I am a good driver. If I do get into a crash, it's because of someone else being a bad driver, or the road being slippery."

A series of experiments reported by Ditto in 1992 found that a core component of the self-serving bias is that information consistent with a preferred conclusion is examined less critically than other types of information. You apply a different standard of proof so that you have a quick glance at information that fits your world view. For example, you are a good driver because you don't have many crashes; you give a long hard look at information that is inconsistent with your preferred conclusion that you are a good driver and don't have crashes rather than it being due to external influences. You will ask questions like "where was the research done?", "how does it apply to me individually", and so on. Your beliefs persist when the alternative is loss of a favourable self-image.

People look for reasons to justify their opinions, being ready to rebuff the challenges of others. Lord et al., in 1979, identified that reasoning is not just used to objectively assess your opinions but to confirm initial views through finding flaws or strengths in any argument. Through a study of people's attitudes towards capital punishment, Lord found that both proponents and opponents of capital punishment rated research that supported their viewpoint as more convincing than the research that did not support their view. This was called a "biased assimilation process". This was irrespective of which belief was held, as long as it supported what they originally thought, people assimilated the new information in a biased manner and ended up more extreme in their beliefs then when they started.

A person's beliefs are difficult to shift. Interesting research examined the different processes that guide judgements of individuals, and found results were consistent with a "bolstering" framework whereby people become invested in their own beliefs or are bolstered when they anticipate debate with others.

Science uses counterfactuals to explore "why"

When cause is confused with effect or when correlation is confused with causation, just because they occur at the same time, we have a problem. It is accepted that a cause is not something that can be seen at the time, that we observe the outcome of the cause, which we may refer to as the "effect". It is difficult to work out a cause, if something does indeed cause the effect, but there are some important things to remember. The first essential part of the difference between cause and effect is that the cause of something must happen before the effect. This seems obvious but it is amazing how often this fundamental aspect is forgotten. The main problem for science is to work out the difference between a cause, and merely something that is associated. Albert Einstein was convinced that one of the greatest achievements of science is the possibility to discover causal relationships by systematic experiment (Floris Cohen, 1994).

Philosophers and scientists have formulated a way of thinking about cause, known as the counterfactual method. Graham will explain, in the box on the following page, how science uses the counterfactual method to do this.

One good thing about science is that all elements of an experiment are identified before the experiment is conducted, thus reducing the chance of other problems with logic, such as identifying causes after the event to explain the outcome, known as ad-hoc reasoning, or changing the criteria of proof to deny a conclusion you don't like. Here we return to confirmation bias (see box entitled "Confirmation bias") where judgements you make are based on your own beliefs despite the evidence to the contrary. Scientific method relies on things being consistent and applying the same rules to both sides of the argument.

"Should" is a word with problems

As Buddhists have declared for centuries, suffering is a part of existence and the cause of suffering is the desire to have things

The weird world of counterfactuals

Science employs something called a counterfactual. Literally "counter to fact", you must use your mind to imagine an identical world to the one you live in, but with one single difference: the thing you believe is a cause of something is removed. Then consider: would the effect still happen, or not? If it does not then you can infer that the effect is being caused by the thing you removed. Obviously this is only in your mind, and the counterfactual world is in your imagination, it is not real. Despite the imaginary nature of this, scientists have designed useful ways to explore causes.

So, how does this help you to work out what a cause of something really is? The best method science has is the randomized controlled trial, often referred to as a drug trial or clinical trial. This is where a study participant is given either the intervention being tested, or a placebo. For example, drug trials use two groups of people, the group who get the drug and a group who do not. This second group is used to replicate a counterfactual world.

and control them. This is described as an attachment to outcome. You may look back on an experience and want it to have ended differently, such as a disagreement leading to an argument for example. A person experiences anger when the reality of the situation, an argument ending badly, doesn't match with their desire to have said things differently or have the other person respond differently. A key word here is "should" – the person gets angry when they think that another person should have acted differently.

When I hear the word "should", I often think of the Ten Command-ments. I see Moses holding the two tablets on Mount Sinai when a person says that the reason they are angry is because someone should have behaved differently or that they were made to be angry by the person – I think "where is the evidence?" The Ten Commandments hold the ethical and spiritual code of conduct for Judaism and Christianity. There are ten of them and they include statements like "you shall not steal" and "you shall not commit murder", which are definitive rules for how people should and shouldn't behave. When we say people should not cut in a line of traffic or take 20 items in the 15-item line at the supermarket, do we really want to add them to the tablets? Those things look heavy enough as it is.

Evaluating your beliefs to help you to explore your "why" questions

You can evaluate your beliefs, as they impact on how and what you think. In many of these situations the confirmation bias comes into play and this makes evaluating your beliefs a difficult process. When you think about information that is relevant to one of your beliefs, you spend more time evaluating it when you disagree with it. When anxious individuals hear information that runs counter to their beliefs, they are less likely to believe it. In one study, it was found that people have difficulty judging information that causes anxiety as fundamentally false (Vroling and de Jong, 2009). Con-versely, reassuring statements are less likely to be seen as true.

Your beliefs about the world and your experiences are maintained without effort, leaving your mind with capacity for more urgent and complex tasks. This works in dangerous situations where immediate reactions are required for safety; you can rely on prior beliefs and act on plausible conclusions without effort. This is opposed to the effort involved in stopping, considering and pondering whether those conclusions meet the high standards of logic. If we had needed to stop and consider whether running was a good idea in the jungle while being chased by a wild tiger, then our ancestors wouldn't have lasted very long.

Biased thinking might not be such a bad thing and might even be helpful in certain areas, for example in improving your self-esteem. Your perception of what is important for any person, such as a virtue or a talent, is biased towards the attributes you already possess. Low achievers in a particular area are likely to perceive the successes of high achievers as exceptional, thereby lessening the shame of their own inability. People think harder and longer about any discouraging test results they receive; they are more inclined to want them to be confirmed and are significantly more sceptical of them. People do not react the same way to test results received by others, however. When research tarnishes the reputation of groups with which people identify, they search for a weakness in the research, such as a statistical loophole for the findings.

This reminds me of a quote, the author of which is not agreed upon. But the adage says that statistics can be used the same way that a drunk person uses a lamp post: more for support than for illumination. So, despite statistics telling you one thing, you may prefer the interpretation that supports your pre-existing belief.

Improving your reasoning

Summarizing the work of Tversky et al. (1988) Mercier showed that, in reasoning, people choose an alternative belief when they can provide a good argument for that choice. This argument can then be used to justify that decision both to themselves as well as to others. Conflict may be useful in helping you to improve your thinking; conflict allows groups to outperform individuals finding solutions to problems that are not seen when there is no dissent within a group. When left to your own devices you will often engage in the Positive Test Strategy, where people suggest ideas that fit with a hypothesis they have already generated. To make an improvement in your reasoning, you need to ask someone else for their opinion. You could say to them "I am getting your opinion on what I plan to do because the book *Feel Good* told me to do so. After doing this I will perform better than going it alone."

This links with science and the scientific method: science is based on falsification and scientists strive to prove things are false. Falsification is useful when the person is in a situation that encourages you to argue against a hypothesis that is not your own. This method can be helpful here when you work on a problem, and you propose a hypothesis and try, in as objective a manner as possible, to prove it wrong.

Hsee (2006) summarized the research in good decision making noting that two aspects, the ability to predict and failure to follow those predictions, were at the heart of poor decision making. In *Blink*, Malcolm Gladwell propounds the idea that complex decisions should be made using our in-built gut reaction: a literal feeling we get within our abdomen. Simpler, less complex questions should be determined using conscious thought according to his thesis. However, there has been stern criticism of these ideas, with evidence supporting and rejecting these notions.

Researchers have identified the difficulties associated with successful change. Heatherton and Nicholls in 1994 found that the difference between successful changes and those that were unsuccessful was that successful individuals often had a reappraisal of life goals and insight. Those able to maintain positive change reported that their identities had changed and their perceptions, temperament, values and goals were affected. This is a distinct difference from the person that says they "can't change" who they are, or they are "too far gone" or it is "too late in life to change".

"Post-it" note technique

As we have seen above there are many words you may use that you should challenge in your thinking. Now start a 3-minute monologue with yourself. Describe yourself *without* using the word "but" or undoing what you've said. Don't cheat and use the word "however", or "nevertheless". On a "post-it" note record every time you do say the word "but" (or similar words). Try this again when you ask yourself why your mood is the way it is during your day.

Chapter 3

ANGER

A *33-year-old artist sat across from me talking about his relationship with a wonderful and supportive partner noting "when I am tired I am guaranteed I am going to wake up in a bad mood; anything anyone says is going to make me snap and say something nasty. I can hold it back in a social situation. It is still there but I can turn it off. It is awful and I hate feeling angry. If she asks me to do something it really irks me. I know it shouldn't. Even when I have got that voice of rationality in my head, the overwhelming emotion is so strong." He looked up sheepishly and seemed to acknowledge what he had to change.*

Sound familiar?

Let's start with a basic statement about anger: anger is normal. The artist is demonstrating a normal range of emotions. If you don't have anger as part of your emotional range, the stimulus you require to stand up for yourself and for others is simply not there. Anger, as an emotional response, may make you feel uncomfortable and it may result in physical symptoms such as your heart racing, your blood feeling like it is boiling and your respiration rate increasing. All of this is within a normal range for your body. As you will see in Chapter 5 "Distress", this is an adaptive response, it is quite normal, and it won't harm you. The problems associated with anger result from a painful process where you feel "You can't make me angry!"

Signs of anger may be complex and difficult to recognize

What is anger? It is a very short word, used extensively in our language, probably with little thought as to what it really means. Anger can be defined as both the result, and the process, of feelings of rage, irritation and annoyance. They most commonly appear as a result of a feeling that you have been wronged or insulted. An important thing to recognize is that when you feel the mood related to being angry, and the emotion anger, these have the same roots as all other emotions. Just like other emotions, the feeling of anger can be seen on a scale: from mild irritation to intense and violent rage.

Often the physiological changes in your body that accompany anger are similar to the "fight or flight response", which Graham describes in the following box. People often talk about anger as a blinding and all-consuming experience, which makes the mood so important to you; it can often feel like you are out of control. Despite this, rest assured your control is still there. This actually gets us to the crux of anger and the problem it poses for you: the perception that someone else made you angry, therefore you are justified in doing what you want in response to having that control "taken away from you".

The fight or flight response

The fight or flight response is a well-understood bodily response that has long been part of the arsenal of survival techniques for all animals. The environment, and the danger it poses, made this response essential for survival. The body actually produces hormones, such as adrenaline, to prepare the body to stand and fight or to leave as quickly as possible, the flight response. Your muscles are given more blood, the heart rate quickens, unnecessary functions slow down. All of these functions ready the body to survive the coming moments. These responses are no longer useful for humans, except in exceptional and rare circumstances.

A renowned psychotherapist, Alfred Adler, worked in Europe in the first few decades of the 20th century and he is known for many advances. His work on anger is summarized below. It notes three strategies in which an aggressive drive is observable and identifiable, which were named by Monte (1995) as:

1. Depreciation – feeling better by describing others as inferior by comparison to your own, "perfect" self.
2. Accusation – blaming others and seeing them as solely responsible for your pain.
3. Self-accusation – attention-seeking behaviour by over-emphasizing your guilt in being solely responsible for your pain.

Note that this is not about the changes in a person's behaviour leading to anger as a result of disease, inherent or acquired biochemistry or neglect. This happens, for example, in a process known as disinhibition in Alzheimer's Disease, or due to extreme violence, a head injury or growth of a tumour. Instead, this is about the experiences of anger that are directed towards others, or yourself, all of which are emotional experiences you are having and which are under your control.

We are social animals so our daily lives involve negotiating and managing anger and frustration-inducing experiences. You may feel emotions such as hurt, fright, disappointment, worry, embarrassment or frustration at what has happened but like a volcano waiting to erupt, your feelings are under the surface. But on eruption of the volcano you may express these feelings as anger.

Anger becomes a problem when you do not manage it

Anger will become a problem for you and those around you when the responses you make are not recognized by you and not managed properly. As with other aspects of mood, preparation, coping statements and using reward are key features to successful mood management. In my clinical work, anger and the consequences of it are common reasons someone chooses to come to see me in the first place. For example I have heard "My wife says I have to control my anger" or "the Judge said 'get yourself under control'". As these quotes illustrate, when anger is not managed well, the results may be problems in relationships or subsequent loss of freedom and further emotional pain.

Anger that you demonstrate reaches further into your life than impacting solely on yourself; it reaches many people around you. Psychologists assess anger by measuring directly observable behaviour like assault, indirect hostility such as breaking things, and verbal hostility, the hurtful things people say. Feeling states are an additional area I look at; feelings where you are irritable, have a negative outlook, stubbornness, resentment and suspicion. When looking at how angry people are perceived by others in their relationships, people often say that the angry person is being "grouchy", "impatient" or "annoyed".

The five predictors of anger

Recently, in 2010, Professor Mahon found that there are five predictors of anger in adolescence that have a significant impact: anxiety, depression, stress, exposure to violence and trait anger. The person's personality, the stresses they experience and the exposures to violence are all important and key to the person's development in relation to anger. You will probably have met someone with trait anger, where the person perceives many situations as annoying, and often you may think that this was an over-reaction. As a person ages, into the critical years of emerging adulthood, expressed anger declines, and factors such as a parent's education and conflict with your parents are important buffers. Expressed anger improves fastest in participants with more educated parents and also for those with greater conflict. These factors provide us with some hope that the situation can be managed.

Men struggle dealing with their anger

The consequences of mood differ markedly between men and women. The evidence is overwhelming that many men have difficulty understanding and expressing their own emotions. Not only do these emotional difficulties get in the way of a man's ability to form and sustain intimate relationships but these difficulties can be limiting and harmful in themselves. The US Centers for Disease Control (CDC) have listed a few of the health and well-being issues faced by men (see box below).

Men's health issues

Men experience poorer general health compared with women. According to the CDC, men:

- die six years earlier than women.
- have a successful suicide rate four times greater than women. In 2006 men aged 35–49 years are now at highest risk.
- are more likely to have Emergency Room visits due to alcohol.
- have an almost four times higher risk of death from homicide than women.

Men don't see their doctor enough and fail to use services in primary care, the gateway to healthcare in most countries, effectively. This is partly due to how men express their symptoms and signs. On the other side of the consultation is the doctor. In one study of General Practitioners' perspectives on health care use by men, doctors believed their male patients received health-related support from their female partners, involving their partners and indirectly addressing their health care needs (Tudiver and Talbot, 1999). Therefore, these patients as a group are taking less responsibility for their health compared to women.

Men's difficulty with emotion is often a secret even to men themselves. Many men, who others view as insensitive, will describe themselves as "loving and caring". Some men will deny an awareness or knowledge of emotion at all and others may display their denial in terms of their masculinity. Men are not taught to have this knowledge and understanding of themselves. Others still will

Men's relationship issues

- The man's complaint that if his wife were more sexually responsive he would feel able to show more affection. This situation usually results in an impasse as the wife views her lack of sexual responsiveness as due to the man's lack of affection = A DEADLOCK.
- The man's belief that they are being "put upon" to show affection the way women do = FRUSTRATION.
- That it is their job to be successful financial providers for the family and to protect them from harm, it is the wife's job to provide for his emotional needs = AN UNREALISTIC RELATIONSHIP.
- Emotions are a waste of time and illogical, what is required most of the time is a solution to some problem = A LIMITED RELATIONSHIP.

simply belittle emotional experience as "soft", "weak" and of no value to men generally. When talking to men about the problems they face, some may respond defensively. For example a suggestion by a partner that they have not been interested in emotional closeness or have not valued the partner by expressing affection can elicit a range of responses. These include examples listed in the box on the previous page.

Men are not listening to the signs their bodies are giving them in relation to their health, accessing healthcare only indirectly and suffering for it with poorer health. I often hear about men not taking responsibility for violence and anger using reasoning such as "I lost control". Men also excuse behaviour with the perceived need for conformity when they say "I had to do it, everyone else was" and the expression of rigid gender roles "it is the way a man is".

Women have more coping mechanisms

Roslyn Corney, a professor of psychology, found that going to the doctor and seeking help was linked to the presence of physical illness. This makes sense. However the presence of psychosocial problems, which are psychological issues embedded within a social context, predicted consultation behaviour in women but not in men. Women were also found to have more confidants and contacted more social agencies than men. Other authors have found that even when consultations for contraception, gynaecological problems and pregnancy were taken into consideration, women of childbearing age consult more than their male counterparts. Women's familiarity with healthcare access may have been generated by the need to consult for contraception, gynaecological problems and pregnancy, but subsequently led to a higher consultation rate for other symptoms.

Recognizing your anger

If you believe in the statement "You can't make me angry" then these types of strategies for you to elicit control and express power are not needed.

It is important to acknowledge that a particular situation you find yourself in, or a behaviour from someone else, has made you angry. Admitting it to yourself is a first step. By identifying triggers to your anger you can prepare for them and identify them before you lose control of the situation. There are many triggers for people, for example, a common one is being in traffic. This has generated a whole type of anger known as "road rage".

The way you respond to your own internal anger often, but not always, corresponds to the degree of anger you are experiencing. People behave angrily by increasing the volume of their voice and changing the tone, trying to convey criticism of the trigger of the anger. Non-verbal behaviours from you, such as being silent when people ask further questions, is one strategy that you may use to deal with anger. Throwing or breaking things and physical violence are other non-verbal expressions. If you behave in this way, then you are angry.

There are strong beliefs around anger, some of which are given in the next box. These beliefs are patently incorrect: anger is a natural and healthy mood to feel at times, and is experienced by people from all walks of life. It is true that excessive anger can lead to a feeling of loss of control but you have the ability to control your anger. Feelings of anger in others do not necessarily mean that you have done something wrong. And this works both ways in that others may not be able, or need, to change their behaviour when you feel angry. A common issue is where someone's anger leads others to believe that any love they had previously experienced has been lost. This does not have to be the case.

Beliefs about anger

- Anger is not OK
- Nice people don't get angry
- I'll lose control if I get angry
- If someone gets angry at me, I must have done something wrong and I am responsible for fixing things
- If I feel angry, they have to change so I don't feel angry anymore
- Anger means I don't love you anymore.

Starting to deal with your anger

Often anger at another person's actions is about the perceptions you have about the other's intent and what you think that person should or shouldn't do. When you delve deeper the rules you apply to others are not always the same as those you apply to yourself. This is a well-known moral debate, often referred to as "The Golden Rule": treat other people the same way you expect to be treated yourself. Or maybe the negative: do not treat others as you do not want to be treated. This Golden Rule recognizes that other people are also an "I" and has been part of cultural and religious norms for many millennia.

Anger management is about developing solutions that you are able to use in the long term. Solutions like avoidance of situations that induce your anger, or avoiding other causes such as alcohol may be very effective in the short term but they fail to stop it happening again. Some useful questions you could ask yourself:

- When was the last time you *didn't* feel angry?
- Does your anger involve emotional, physical or psychological abuse?

- Does your anger lead to problems with personal relationships and work?
- Are you using alcohol or other drugs to try to feel better?

Some people believe that venting anger is beneficial. However, if you hold that belief you are more likely to become angry to try to solve your mood problems. This is especially true in young men. By expressing your true feelings, whether they are guilt, anger or frustration, in a more structured and controlled way, you can avoid repressing the emotion, release some of your underlying feelings, and do something directly about what is making you angry.

But I don't get angry!

Saying or thinking that is OK but as we have already said anger is normal. You may mean I don't have problems with anger. However just like any other emotion or mood, understanding your anger and why it happens is an important exercise that might not be important for you but might help others. Think for a moment how you can learn and practise better ways of expressing anger. What are the things you can do to decrease the likelihood of anger getting out of control?

Start with a list of the various things that are triggers for you and another list of the warning signs of your anger:

- Can you recognize these situations easily?
- What are your body's warning signs of anger?
- What are the strategies you already use for managing anger?
- When you are angry are there certain thinking styles which can lead to exaggerated and irrational thoughts?
- Are you jumping to conclusions or taking something personally that has little or nothing to do with you?

Dealing with anger by looking for patterns and applying logic

How do you feel about what is happening? Talking to others can be helpful during the early stages of feeling angry. Sometimes it can help you to write things down. Writing about these feelings and sensations can sometimes help give you some distance and perspective. It helps you to understand your feelings, identify solutions for changing your situation and improve your management of your mood.

How you make sense of the situation is important here. Using our example of heavy traffic, and feelings of rage, you could say to yourself "I have handled worse traffic than this". This is a way of reframing your experience by putting it in a broader perspective of all the traffic you have ever experienced.

The fundamental aspect to dealing with anger is to change your view on the situation of the other person that is making you feel angry. There are particular thinking styles often used in anger management. CBT works well as discussed in Chapter 1 "How are you?". When a person holds a rigid view of the world, then any violation of their world view is a direct challenge to their opinion and view of themselves. You are going to defend a view if it has this kind of importance to you. When you have a mode of thinking that holds other people responsible for your pain, distress or mistakes, then anger is a consequence. If you think you are controlled by someone else, you might view yourself as a helpless and hopeless victim. A good example "if only my wife would place the wet towel in the basket rather than on the bed, I would be happier". Giving up your responsibility for managing your mood is seen in the belief "I'll lose control if I get angry". Just because you have a particularly intense emotion doesn't remove your personal responsibility for your words and actions.

Other generalizations can occur when you see a single event as one of a never-ending list of things that have gone against you. When you argue, do you use words such as "always" or "never"? These words are typical of over-generalizations. Parents with teenagers often hear these words, such as "everyone stays up until midnight" or "nobody does their homework".

Often we try to look for a hero and a villain in our dealings with others. This is an example of black and white, or all or nothing, thinking. When your experiences are viewed as one extreme or another there are no shades of grey or middle ground. You may end up condemning others on the basis of a single event. For example the estate agent that sold my last house was bad at his job; therefore I never want to move house again as all estate agents are rubbish.

"Post-it" note technique

This seems a good time to introduce the first "post-it" note technique for this chapter. Think of a situation when you felt angry and write this down on a "post-it" note. You could write down a single word that reminds you of this, or you could write a few sentences describing it. This is up to you.

Are you able to look at this situation in an alternative way? It will now be helpful for you to write down this alternative. This will reinforce your knowledge that situations are not always as they first appear.

Using considered argument may work

You may wish to change the views of a person you are talking to and there are tools to do this, such as using argument: we described these in Chapter 2 "Challenge your thinking", in the box entitled "Principles of logic". Employing an argument, arguing if you will, is an essential skill and, when taught well, is the basis for critical thinking and sound reasoning; how you persuade someone and justify argument is a good reflection of how you think. The way you evaluate your own conclusions can help challenge your beliefs and those of others. This is not to encourage arguing as a release of anger, but rather as a way of you getting better at managing your emotions of frustration and ultimately anger.

CBT research and its usefulness in managing anger are divided into three areas: cognitive preparation, skill development and training. In a meta-analysis of more than 1,600 subjects, a wide range of subjects receiving CBT treatment were significantly better off in how they reported managing their anger compared to those that didn't. This type of treatment involves using insight to gain an understanding of the triggers for anger as we discussed earlier in the chapter. Let's start with some basic techniques that can help in looking at our thoughts in a different way.

Successful mood management

Preparation, coping and reward are key aspects of your success-ful anger management. Preparation will help you to react appro-priately when you need a coping mechanism. Trying to make a plan while you are angry will lead to further problems and ulti-mately defeat. Make a list of things to say to yourself before you get angry or the things you can do to make it less likely that you will get angry in a given situation. When you are attempting to cope with an anger trigger, focus on managing the situation. Don't focus on what other people are saying or should be doing.

For preparation: say to yourself "I'll be able to do this. It might get
    difficult, but I have a plan."
Coping: Say to yourself "Stay calm, relax, and breathe . . ."
Reward: Say to yourself "I managed that really well."

Some of the plans you prepare may need you to make use of "time out", distraction or relaxation. Time out is a tried and tested technique for handling relationship issues of all kinds. It requires you to notice emotions building up, labelling them correctly and then acting on them. If you notice the feeling of anger getting out of control, leave the situation and take time out. You should suspend the argument for another time. Try removing yourself from the situation, stepping out of the room, or even going for a walk. During this time away, plan how you are going to stay calm when your situation resumes, identify any alternatives available and look at what is the most important outcome from this situation. Always come back from your time out: don't resign yourself to the situation and see the outcome as inevitable. Time out only works to build trust if you come back calmer, at the agreed time and are able to hear what the other person has to say. If not, take another time out until you are able to return.

Distraction is a useful and multi-purpose strategy for managing anger. Try to distract your mind from the situation, person or behaviour that is making you angry. Count to ten. Backwards. In Spanish. You get my point. Play soothing music or talk to a friend about the situation you are experiencing anger about. By taking the edge off the strong physical and emotional sensations, you are better able to identify the unhelpful thinking styles and beliefs which distort thinking.

Relaxation uses the same components of distraction with the benefit of initiating the relaxation or calming response. Relaxation strategies reduce the feelings of tension and stress, and your body reacts accordingly. Strategies such as taking slow, long deep breaths, counting on the in and out-breaths, and watching your belly rise and fall, are great ways to distract and relax your mind. This allows the stress hormones to dissipate and release the muscles that have become wound up and constricted. Some of these techniques are developed further in Chapter 10 "Relaxation techniques".

Be assertive and get your needs met

You can learn assertiveness skills which allow your anger to be expressed in clear and respectful ways. Practising saying things in an assertive way is a great way to manage anger. Assertiveness reflects the belief that all people are equal and therefore entitled to feelings and rights. When you are assertive, there is clarity with others about what you understand as their needs and wants, and you feel okay about your own feelings. Respect is an important component here: both respecting the other person's rights and your own. Again this returns to the issue of using absolute terms which we discussed in relation to generalizations. Absolute terms like "should" or "never" or "always", for example "You're always doing that!" are statements that are almost always inaccurate (see what I did there). Absolute terms attempt to justify your reasoning, and don't give you or the other person any options. Your approach is best avoiding these terms.

When you first start a relationship you can identify the things you have gratitude about very easily. However, this can deteriorate over time and annoyance and anger starts to develop. Communication is important here. You could try the exercise for communication shown in the following box:

Communication exercise

Give the following a try:

Say "I feel" (emotion)
    "when you" (behaviour)
    "because" (reason)
    "I would like (the option the person has).

For example "I feel happy when you make me breakfast because it makes me feel loved. I would like you to make me breakfast every day" or alternatively "I feel frustrated when you leave the wet towel on the bed because I don't feel listened to as I have told you before. I would like you to hang it up in the bathroom."

The examples given in the box provide the basis of assertive communication. Identifying how you feel means that you are taking responsibility for the type of feelings and their intensity. You are also pinning down emotions that can sometimes be quite nebulous and uncertain, those things under the surface of the volcano. Hearing or reading the words which describe how you feel can establish greater insight and offers a different perspective to how you experience the words. You are not just hearing them in your head but spoken aloud.

Offering an explanation to someone does improve the outcome

When you identify a behaviour in someone else you help them recognize that this is something that is separate from them and related to a specific event in time; your mood is not changing because they did something three years ago but you are letting them know that the change in mood is related to a specific event that you are discussing now.

Providing a reason to a person that has been the recipient of your anger lets them know that you have thought about the mood change and that it has a basis. You explain to them that you are not getting upset at the person because they are a Capricorn or their favourite colour is blue. Your change in mood is related to the meaning of an event, the importance this has for you, and you are sharing that with them. By ending the assertive statement above with "I would like . . ." you provide the person with an option.

The goal of this communication method is the expression of emotion with respect; whatever the outcome; by being assertive in this way you are achieving this goal of respectful communication. If the other person you are using assertive communication with decides to change, or indeed not to change, their behaviour, it is very much up to them and by being assertive you are respecting that. The benefit to you is that you gain more information from the exchange and this can inform what you do from here on.

Dealing with another person's anger

The identification of responsibility is a major component of successful mood management. I talk about its importance in the chapter on self-esteem and here it takes on some significance. When a person is being abusive or angry towards another, it often says more about the abuser than the abused. This is increasingly becoming part of the collective experience of people generally, as found in the phrase "What is your problem?" as a reaction to being confronted with an angry person.

Porcupine dilemma

A number of porcupines huddled together for warmth on a cold day in winter; but, as they began to prick one another with their quills, they were obliged to disperse. However the cold drove them together again, when just the same thing happened. At last, after many turns of huddling and dispersing, they discovered that they would be best off by remaining at a little distance from one another. In the same way the need of society drives the human porcupines together, only to be mutually repelled by the many prickly and disagreeable qualities of their nature. The moderate distance which they at last discover to be the only tolerable condition of intercourse, is the code of politeness and fine manners; and those who transgress it are roughly told – in the English phrase – to keep their distance. By this arrangement the mutual need of warmth is only very moderately satisfied; but then people do not get pricked. A man who has some heat in himself prefers to remain outside, where he will neither prick other people nor get pricked himself (by Schopenhauer in 1851).

The responsibility to take power and control back is yours. As in politics, power is never given away, it has to be taken. As I have described with the feelings associated with unhappiness, you may find that negative events are internalized. When dealing with an angry person, you need to externalize the cause of the distress and not take responsibility for the other person's behaviour. Just as this chapter began by stating "you can't make me angry", so too you can't be responsible for another person's anger. It is their choice and their behaviours are their responsibility. In leading a healthy life you need to define which behaviours are acceptable and if this person is violating that boundary, then you have to be clear and hand back the responsibility to the person for their behaviour. In your life you will be presented with many invitations to take responsibility for other people's behaviour; however it is up to you to draw a line in the sand and act when this is crossed.

"Post-it" note technique

This "post-it" note technique will involve noticing things that make you feel good and expressing them. As I mentioned above you need to notice good and bad feelings and this helps you to become able to identify when this occurs in your day and even change your day for the better.

Each day for the next week, identify something you feel gratitude for and write it down using the same technique as I described in the box entitled "Communication exercise". If possible say it to the person who helped you feel this.

"I feel . . .", "when you . . .", "because . . .". "I would like . . ."

In the second week, start another "post-it" note and identify the things that are causing you grief or frustration. Use the same technique and write down the things that are causing you frustration, from the big to the small. Again if possible say them to the person causing them. The results will surprise you.

By practising assertive communication, you can reinforce the boundaries you have developed and make being consistent a part of how you are in the world. You are looking to improve the chances of you acting in accordance with your values, identifying unhelpful beliefs about control and power while practising the skills that respect your needs and the needs of others.

Chapter 4

SELF-EFFICACY

A 30-year-old mother of two who, just like 15% of childbearing women, suffered from postnatal depression, described how pervasive the feelings can be: "I felt like the postnatal depression had introduced doubt in every area of my life. From doubting my ability as a mother, wife, sister, daughter and friend to doubting others' feelings for me. My days were filled with anxiety that at any moment everything, and everyone, that I love would be taken from me by methods that I could not control."

Self-efficacy is your belief in your own capability to produce the outcomes you want. It is how you perceive that you are able to produce a level of performance, a level with which you are comfortable. This, therefore, is your ability to exercise influence over events. The events we refer to here are those that affect your life, that impact on your well-being and on your relationships. You have undoubtedly heard the term self-esteem used. We will deal with the issue of self-esteem – a person's evaluation of their own worth – in Chapter 8 "Self-esteem". But self-esteem is slightly different to self-efficacy. In this chapter we will discuss accessible ideas around the impact self-esteem has on you and the way you can develop and improve your self-efficacy.

Your self-efficacy determines how you feel, think, and ultimately how you behave. How does this happen? Difficult aspects of your life can be dealt with in different ways. One of these ways, which is known as integration, is where these aspects of your life are systematically completed and accepted as part of your life story. An opposing way to deal with difficult situations would be for you to feel fear and subsequently avoid these situations. Seeing yourself as successful with attempts to deal with difficult tasks helps to motivate you further. These successes also generate a sense of engagement with yourself in that activity.

A common problem is for people to think that acceptance is only about the successes. But acceptance of failure is equally important. Indeed, it has been said that learning to fail is one of the most important life skills that should be developed in young people. When you experience a failure, whilst making an attempt at succeeding, it helps to build your resilience. In this respect, resilience describes your ability to cope with stress and adversity. This characteristic has been recognized as essential in the world's great leaders. Resilience will allow you to maintain your efforts when a task becomes difficult, and help you to try again when you have been prevented from completing the task. Starting again at tackling a given task is not a case of you being in denial about the world, but rather attributing failure to things you can control. These things may be due to many different reasons such as an insufficient degree of effort, the need for you to get more knowledge about a subject, or the requirement to develop and learn a new skill. As you will see from Chapter 5 "Distress", your resilience reduces the chance of developing distress and reduces the feelings of stress generally.

"Post-it" note technique

Every evening for the next week, write down something that you have done well, completed to the level you hoped. This could be anything, something simple such as making a nice meal, something that you completed in your job, tidying a cupboard that has long needed some attention. On the "post-it" note write "I have had a success today because . . ." and complete this sentence.

Psychological changes can be explained through changes in self-efficacy

Self-efficacy is seen as feeding your ability to cope, where you can use the skills you acquire in different environments, against different stressors in the future. The theory behind self-efficacy looks to explain, and then predict, psychological changes achieved by different types of treatment. These aim to improve your well-being and health and the changes, or outcomes, will lead to improvements in your coping mechanisms. A fundamental aspect of this theory is that it increases whatever psychology does, it increases the range and strength of skills you can draw on.

The psychological changes that may come about through changes to self-efficacy are seen as important as they are seen to relate to your expectations of personal self-efficacy and determine whether you initiate a coping behaviour. Once you start to use a strategy, you must be aware of how much effort will be expended, and how long you will be able to sustain this in the face of obstacles and adverse experiences. Exposure to activities that look threatening but are in fact relatively safe, and the persistence with which these are maintained, can be used to learn, achieve and maintain resilience. These experiences then add to self-efficacy with the corresponding reductions in avoidance or defensive behaviour as products of successful integration.

An opposing method to integration is avoidance, and reducing the use of avoidant behaviours is important: stress is often generated by the interaction of such avoidance experiences, which we discuss in Chapter 5 "Distress". If you engage in passive problem solving where you allow things to resolve by themselves without active involvement, you are doing a less than perfect job of problem solving. It is the closest thing to giving up, ironically without taking responsibility for giving up. If you have little motivation to solve a problem and if you do attempt a solution and give little energy to the task, you often end your involvement as soon as possible.

Unfortunately this type of behaviour – a lack of involvement – makes it more likely that there will be a negative outcome from the lack of skillful effort you have given. For example, when you are given a challenging task, such as one you may come across at work, you might have some initial difficulties completing the task, and in the end totally give up on it. This means your self-efficacy suffers. If you think you cannot handle this and it is beyond your capabilities, you will probably fail. This may also lead you to be more likely to avoid a similar situation in the future.

This avoidance may lead you to ask yourself "what is the point in trying?" You are more likely to put minimal effort into the task and became very frustrated and give up prematurely. Avoidance of the challenging task is another way to lower self-efficacy and not give you a chance to succeed. Procrastination is often a symptom here, which in psychology is a description of a person's behaviour when they do a low-priority action instead of a high-priority action. This is often because the lower priority action is easier to accomplish or is more fun. Graham, for example, says that whenever he has difficult things to achieve, he has the cleanest house in his town. Anything to avoid the difficult work.

A renowned psychologist, Albert Bandura, who is a professor at Stanford University in the USA, developed a model of self-efficacy. In this model, the expectations you have of your personal efficacy are derived from four principal sources of information: performance accomplishments, vicarious experience, verbal persuasion and physiological states. Performance accomplishments are things that you have achieved, that you have completed or done well in. Vicarious experience refers to an experience someone else has, but you gain from their experience. On an everyday level you often experience situations vicariously whilst you watch the television, or read a novel. Verbal persuasion is what you hear other people talking about, telling you, whilst chatting, discussing or arguing. And your physiological state, touched upon in Chapter 1 "How are you?", is what is happening to your body, the state within which your body lies and the functions that go on all the time in your body.

This model has been explored by scientists, and Bandura and Locke published a paper in 2003 that looked at the evidence from nine studies of behavioural functioning at work, school, with sport, health and psychosocial functioning. Self-efficacy was found to be a strong predictor of the level of performance, coping behaviours, and perseverance. Your belief in your self-efficacy gets you going and keeps you going.

Overall health and self-efficacy are linked

Let's look at some examples that can affect health. Postpartum, or postnatal, depression is a severe condition that develops after the birth of a child, and can affect any mother, and sometimes the father, following the birth of their child. Although the exact causes are not known and obvious changes in hormone levels affect mood, there are many other factors at play. There are physical changes to the body after giving birth, work and social relationships can deteriorate and sleep deprivation is common. Sleep is a very important component of your nutrition and this will be explored in more detail in Chapter 10 "Relaxation techniques". The worries about your ability to be a good mother are important too.

Self-efficacy associated with feelings of being a parent have been studied, and found to increase over time. From a common sense perspective, the benefits of previous experience, with an increase in the number of children, increase your self-efficacy. In this respect, you have witnessed your ability to successfully raise a child. A vicarious social support, where you derive confidence and contentment through the experience of others, and direct social support are protective against postnatal depression. Parenting satisfaction and marital satisfaction are associated with better outcomes also. Conversely a negative relationship between maternal and parental self-efficacy are linked to maternal stress, anxiety and postpartum depression.

Chronic disease self-management programmes are education programmes designed to help people improve their confidence and self-efficacy to better manage chronic conditions like asthma and diabetes. It builds on the fact that each day people with chronic diseases take care of their food and fluid intake; they might exercise and take their medication and in doing so they choose to reduce stress and generally pursue well-being. In these ways they are self-managing their illness.

As part of the programme a person is given some written documentation that allows them to manage their disease better. For example, if a person has diabetes this documentation may say that if your glucose levels go above a threshold, you should seek advice from your healthcare professional. Your diabetes specialist nurse may advise increasing your insulin. People who use these programmes aim to:

- be better informed about their condition and various treatment options available,
- plan their care and review that plan,
- increase activities that are protective and promote health,

- monitor and manage the signs and symptoms relating to the disease,
- lessen the impact of a patient's condition on physical functioning, emotions and interpersonal relationships.

The programs are successful and have effects on health behaviours, physical and psychological health status, and health care utilization. Ultimately self-efficacy improves as the person integrates their achievements and failures in managing their disease.

As you are all aware, there is a real concern about obesity in adults, and increasingly in children. It leads to many problems, such as heart disease, diabetes and cancer. As such, the World Health Organization has identified obesity as one of the major global threats to public health. Self-efficacy is an important mediator for helping obese patients initiate and maintain the physical activity interventions that are critical to weight loss. Prevention is better than cure and for those in the healthy weight range, behavioural interventions are important for improving self-efficacy and for physical activity.

Success in education and your professional life relies on self-efficacy

In 2001, Judge and Bono published a paper which found that self-efficacy is the most important factor in determining our job satisfaction, and job performance, when compared to self-esteem or emotional stability. In education, self-efficacy predicts the motivation and learning of a student. As an essential ingredient to learning, it predicts outcome, such as students' activity choices, effort, persistence and emotional reactions. These ingredients are then mediated by self-efficacy which leads to better academic achievement.

The school years are a crucial formative period in people's lives. School and college, through to university and continuing professional development, function as a setting where your skills and knowledge are tested. Your competency is continually tested, evaluated, and there is plenty of social comparison. Graham and I have both taught many school and university-level students. We have seen how students benefit hugely from learning, with the associated increases in self-efficacy extending beyond the lecture hall or classroom. We also know that those who are able to believe in themselves to create and succeed are students who will likely succeed.

As described previously there are many ways in which your biases interrupt the process where you compare yourself to others. These biases in your expectations, as covered in Chapter 2 "Challenge your thinking" particularly, will skew your integration of new information. The comparison that occurs in groups can be an advantage as it can raise the perception of your capability by taking away the perceived variability that exists between you and other people – in other words you feel more "normal". By using cooperative learning where the team works together towards an academic or other goal, and the success of the team is paramount, the team's objectives help you to promote more positive self-evaluations. Individualistic processes, and the competition these can engender, get in the way of good outcomes.

You can make progress by using learning activities

Interventions that aim to increase self-efficacy have the effect of increasing positive behaviours. The very things mentioned about feedback on your past or indeed others' performance, allowing for vicarious experience, produce the highest levels of self-efficacy according to a paper published by Ashford and colleagues in 2010. This is what is known in science as a meta-analysis. This is where all of the studies on a subject are put together to make a powerful set of evidence. Vicarious experience was associated with higher levels of self-efficacy while aspects like persuasion, graded mastery and identification of barriers were associated with lower levels of self-efficacy.

A really useful tool I use is to guide people through mastery exercises which are a powerful way to improve coping by action. In these exercises you perceive that you have "mastered" something, such as an activity or a skill. For example, people with intense apprehension and phobias are simply engaging in self-protective reactions, and the aim of therapy is to build coping skills. These help to strengthen your belief that you can control your reaction to these threats, and these will allow you to expose yourself further to the stressors. Graded exposure exercises help do this, as they allow you to realize that you can perform these behaviours successfully, often despite yourself and your thinking. People who successfully change are more likely to report control over a specific behaviour than people who do not change. As we will see in Chapter 6 "Unhappiness", the importance of blaming external events for failures is critical as it is associated with successful change.

In such situations I use the door as an analogy to explain the rationale behind graded exposure. First of all imagine you have an intense phobia about getting closer to a door: this may have come about because of the fear of getting your fingers jammed in the hinge and the pain that undoubtedly will cause. Now as you get closer to the stressor, the door, the intensity of your fear increases.

The opposite is also true, the further you move away from the door the lower your fear. This increase and decrease in fear by moving closer to, and further from, the stressor is important. It provides a gradient, or hill, for you to climb up every time you get closer to the door. Once you are up the hill, which is difficult but achievable, there is an easy way to get away from the door, which is metaphorically downhill. You feel better, at least less distressed, when you get away from the door.

The analogy now moves up a gear as you have the dilemma of how to get out of the room that the door protects; in the analogy the window is the only alternative. This is a painful route as there are rose bushes just outside the window. This route is hard for you to use as it is difficult to twist your body through the window and avoid the thorns. But, despite this, you do it as the door terrifies you. You feel less distressed the further you get away from the door, and after a while you get pretty flexible at getting through the window. Unfortunately you don't get any good at getting through doors, and your lock-picking skills are getting worse and worse the more you avoid this door.

In this analogy, progress is made through identifying the feared activity, showing that others can get through it, identifying the skills required to get through it and then breaking these activities down into more manageable steps. Experiencing the risk in these feared activities for a short period, then rewarding the progress made is important. Your self-efficacy increases as you move closer to the door, use the window to escape less frequently and increase the range and diversity of coping strategies to deal with the distress. These activities will make the coping mechanisms more generalizable to other fears that may also be playing a part in reducing your self-efficacy.

"Post-it" note technique

From the first note, you will have written down something you have completed well. Now take a second "post-it" note, and write down one thing that did not go as well as you had hoped. Be honest and accept what happened. Have you learnt anything from this? How could you have done something differently?

Seeing and hearing someone else succeed increases your self-efficacy

In my work, I often perform activities with a person that they initially fear. In a broader way we are creating and strengthening self-efficacy through vicarious experience. As shown earlier in relation to postnatal depression and social support networks, vicarious experience reinforces the thought "if they can do it, I can do it". Seeing others similar to you succeed by their sustained effort raises your belief that you possess the capabilities to do what you require to succeed.

Verbal persuasion can also be a powerful way to improve self-efficacy. When you accept that people can be trusted you are more likely to believe that you possess the capabilities to achieve your planned activities when others tell you that you can. You are more likely to bolster your efforts and sustain them even when problems do arise. Unfortunately you must be careful using this approach, as it seems easier to reduce self-efficacy when verbal persuasion is given in a malevolent way to make you feel worse.

Positive outcomes are harder to achieve through verbal persuasion alone.

Physiological states can improve a belief in yourself

Stressful events are accompanied by changes in your body. You may feel nervous with "butterflies in my stomach" for example. People who have high self-efficacy are more likely to view this state of physical arousal as useful, giving them the energy required to perform.

Graham and I have experienced feelings in response to the stressful events in our jobs. Having been required to speak at large conferences, to large lecture theatres with many hundreds of people were often effective triggers for a stress response. Beforehand I felt nervous, had sweaty palms and my stomach was full of butterflies. I know that this is a normal physiological response, and that everybody has these nerves. Using this knowledge allowed me to perform well, and not to feel that I was different from anyone else.

Early in Graham's career speaking to groups of people filled him with horror. He spent a simple morning with a group of others who had the same feelings. Gifted teachers who focus on improving public speaking skills often use a house brick. The tutor passed the house brick around the group. They felt its weight, how cumbersome it felt and difficult to control, how it affected their balance and their muscles. This was a demonstration that we all felt the same thing, the same weight, the same awkwardness, and this included our experienced tutor giving the session. This has really helped Graham to realize we are all the same, we all feel the same, and there is no need to feel picked on, or victimized, or specifically disadvantaged. The important point here is to manage these physical feelings limiting how they interfere with your performance.

These experiences, and both the successes and failures in dealing with them, have increased our self-efficacy. It is not a process that ends, but we continue to work on ourselves to maintain the levels of performance we wish to achieve.

Those with self-doubts and a concern about their ability regard their arousal as a debilitating force. A misattribution of arousal is often the case here, for example in people suffering from panic attacks where uncertainty becomes a negative feedback loop. This is the process whereby the person mistakenly assumes what is causing them to feel aroused is that something very bad is about to happen, for example a heart attack. Often this feeling is just a normal variation in everyday physiological sensations. The symptoms of heart disease are breathlessness, chest pain and palpitations around physical exertion. However the symptoms associated with panic attacks often occur at rest, and seem to get worse the more you focus on them. The feedback loop comes when you think you could faint, and this in itself has a physiological impact, increasing your heart rate and a feeling of breathlessness which worries you more, which focuses your attention on what could be about to go wrong which takes you into a cycle of concern. And so on and so forth.

Relaxation as self-efficacy

There are many aspects to relaxation training that can influence your self-efficacy. Relaxation is about letting go. For individuals whose personalities are more rigid, emotionally unstable, or not open to new experiences, the feelings associated with the relaxation response are initially very scary. Feeling heavy, or indeed like you are falling, trigger the fear responses of agitation and you are especially prone to this if they are new experiences. These sensations might resemble a panic attack, however as we have noted above, these are normal physiological changes and cannot be stopped by conscious thought or will.

The desire to always be in control is the area where people can practise letting go, falling into relaxation. By desensitizing yourself to stress you also know what is required when you need to be energized, focused and attentive. These skills allow you to build up the stress response as well as being able to dial it back. You'll find more information on relaxation strategies in Chapter 10 "Relaxation techniques".

Improving your self-efficacy

Self-efficacy is the belief a person has in their capability to exercise control over how they function and the things that affect their lives. The impact of these beliefs influences life choices, motivation, outcomes and resilience to adversity. People's beliefs in their own efficacy are developed in four areas. These include vicarious experiences, seeing people similar to you manage demands successfully. The persuasion from others that you have the capabilities to succeed. That it feels right and your senses are telling you where your strengths and vulnerabilities are. People change over their lives and therefore recharge their sense of self-efficacy to sustain the effort required to get to where they want to go.

Positive psychology is different from the focus on deficit and labelling of thoughts as unhelpful and looks to increase positive emotion, engagement and meaning in a person's life. In one study, it was found that effects lasted more than six months and remission rates were higher than treatment as usual and also those patients who supplemented treatment with medication (Seligman et al., 2006). As we will see in Chapter 6 "Unhappiness", low mood, poor self-efficacy and little motivation can initiate and maintain poor moods.

Chapter 5
DISTRESS

A mother of three, Julie had experienced anxiety before but she was looking at it from a different angle now. She noted her avoidance over the years. "Being in my bathers I feel self-conscious because I am exposed and vulnerable; I can't hide. Jumping in the pool, although cold and wet, gives me a place to hide. It hides the bits I don't want to show. If I have to walk along the stands where people are swimming and I am in my bathers I have two choices. I can be brave and continue walking or I can get in the cold pool. I always go for jumping in and hiding; I know the 'terrible' in the pool because I have done it before."

Distress is an emotional state which you may find yourself in when you are unable to deal with stress. Stress is defined as your body's response to something that you experience in your environment. In this way, stress is a completely normal part of your life and is not in itself a bad thing. In fact, people perform better with some level of stress because, as you will see, the stress response makes you more alert and helps you to concentrate better. This is sometimes known as eustress. The cause or object leading to the stress is known as a "stressor". The Yerkes-Dodson law of performance, illustrated below, shows that a little stress brings out the best

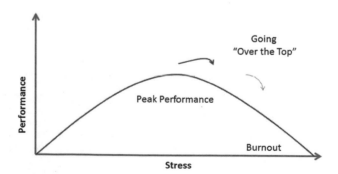

Figure 5.1: Yerkes-Dodson law of performance

performance. But you may rapidly deteriorate in performance when stress becomes too much.

Distress results when your physical, psychological or behavioural well-being is challenged, and can create feelings of worry, uneasiness or even fear. Given it is often hard to pin down these emotions, there are many words people use to describe these feelings, with some of them given in the box below. Do any of these sound familiar to you?

Feelings associated with anxiety

Absent-minded, Afflicted, Afraid, Aggravated, Aggressive, Agonized, Alarmed, Alert, Alive, Angst, Annoyed, Anxiety, Anxious, Apprehension, Awkward, Bothered, Bottled up, Boxed in, Breathless, Broken up, Caged, Cautious, Challenged, Combative, Concern, Conflicted, Crazy, Defensive, Discomfort, Disquiet, Disturbed, Divided, Eager, Ecstatic, Edgy, Fear, Fearful, Fretful, Frightened, Hassled, Impatient, Jittery, Jumpy, Nervousness, Pressured, Scared, Strained, Stress, Tense, Terrified, Troubled, Unease, Worry, Wound up.

Distress and fear are components of the medical conditions known as the "anxiety disorders", more commonly referred to as "anxiety". These include generalized anxiety disorder, phobia, panic and obsessive compulsive disorder. Distress may be brought on by a major life event such as chronic illnesses or financial concerns but many people suffer from stress without such a trigger. We can learn a lot from the scientific and clinical work done in this area, and throughout this chapter we will use the advances made in the treatment of anxiety to help deal with problems associated with distress.

The stress response, once it has started, is one of those things we can stop. In anxiety management, knowledge is power: the knowledge you can wield about your own body and the risks you face in the world are the most important tools to help stop situations becoming distressing. This knowledge will also make sure that situations are managed so that they don't go any further than they need to. This is why you will spend some time identifying things you can change and those you can't.

In a funny sketch by the American deadpan comedian Bob Newhart, a doctor continually shouts "Stop it!" at his patient, with a slightly frightening end (see the box below). In order to stop anxiety, there is plenty you need to understand about it – not just to say "Stop it!" to yourself. This chapter describes the components, physical, behavioural and psychological, of distress and the thoughts, feelings and actions required to achieve successful treatment. When you experience these sensations, and become better at recognizing them, you will learn that they are not harmful or dangerous. This also opens up the opportunity that will allow you to make it work *for* you rather than against you. We discuss this opportunity further in Chapter 10 "Relaxation techniques".

Bob Newhart sketch "Stop it!"

KATHERINE: I'm Katherine Bigmans. Janet Carlisle referred me.
After a little discussion on billing . . .
DR. SWITZER: Tell me about the problem that you wish to address.
KATHERINE: Oh, okay. Well, I have this fear of being buried alive in a box. I just start thinking about being buried alive and I begin to panic.
DR. SWITZER: Has anyone ever tried to bury you alive in a box?

KATHERINE: No. No, but truly thinking about it does make my life horrible. I mean, I can't go through tunnels or be in an elevator or in a house, anything boxy.

DR. SWITZER: So, what you are saying is you are claustrophobic?

KATHERINE: Yes, yes, that's it.

DR. SWITZER: All right. Well, let's go, Katherine. I'm going to say two words to you right now. I want you to listen to them very, very carefully. Then I want you to take them out of the office with you and incorporate them into your life.

A little more banter . . .

DR. SWITZER: Okay. Here they are. Stop it!

KATHERINE: I'm sorry?

DR. SWITZER: Stop it!

KATHERINE: Stop it?

DR. SWITZER: Yes. S-T-O-P, new word, I-T.

Katherine goes on to explain she washes her hands too much, has bulimia, she has self-destructive relationships with men, and she is afraid to drive.

DR. SWITZER: What's the problem, Katherine?

KATHERINE: I don't like this. I don't like this therapy at all. You are just telling me to stop it.

DR. SWITZER: And you don't like that?

KATHERINE: No, I don't.

DR. SWITZER: So you think we are moving too fast, is that it?

KATHERINE: Yes. Yes, I do.

DR. SWITZER: All right. Then let me give you ten words that I think will clear everything up for you. You want to get a pad and a pencil for this one? . . . Here are the ten words: Stop it or I'll bury you alive in a box!

Sketch ends

You feel a response to stress in your body

Knowing and understanding the physiology behind the stress response is one of the most important aspects to managing distress. Stress is nebulous, it is unclear and hazy, and your job is to recognize it for what it is. This allows us to chart where it starts and where it ends. The terrain, hills and valleys of this map are important, as experiences vary in severity from mild tension to full-blown panic. The stress response can be a brief flush, over in a few seconds, through to a pervasive mindset that colours the world and is a constant companion.

Everyone has experienced some amount of stress in their lives whether it be taking an exam or hearing a sudden noise when you are alone in a dark house. How do you know this is a stress response? Well, our body recognizes sensations such as dizziness, numbness, and being short of breath. As you become more aware of your body you may notice your own warning signs. Take a look at the next box – perhaps you can identify one or more of them as being something you have experienced? This list is not exhaustive, there are many different signs that you may become aware of.

Anxiety warning signs

- Tension in your forehead or shoulders
- Sensations of nausea, lightness in your stomach or breathing more rapidly
- Things you do, like picking your nails or clenching your fists
- Noticing events, such as becoming more angry more quickly
- Noticing feelings of impatience, frustration and being more upset with people more often

Distress also does not have to develop rapidly, or acutely. It can develop slowly. Although not strictly true, the story of the frog in the pot is a good description of the effects of chronic stress. The poor frog in our story is placed in boiling water and we figure it will jump out to escape the distress. The twist here is that if the frog is placed in cold water that is slowly heated to boiling, it will not escape and attempt to cope with the danger but will be cooked to death. When dealing with distress this highlights your inability to react to significant changes when they occur gradually.

These sensations are important for survival

Every animal has a stress response to a perceived threat, when they think they are in danger. The response, called the fight/flight response, touched on briefly in Chapter 3 "Anger", prepares you for a fight with another animal or alternatively to run away from a predator to feel safe again. Without this protection mechanism, humans would have not survived.

The fight/flight response is automatic. It stops our mind thinking and allowing reasoning to get in the way of a quick response. We take action. In today's world, in developed societies, it is required less often but it is still essential that when we are confronted by something that will harm us we act quickly. Graham explains a little more about what your body does and how this makes you feel in the box on the following page.

When you are stressed, your heart beats more quickly which may make it feel as though it will "leave my chest". This is an important part of the response, so that the oxygen the muscles require for action will be there. The downside is that you might look pale when stressed, feel light headed and notice your hands becoming tingly. A tightness in your chest is associated with the stress response. Often when you get frightened the rapid intake of breath is the first audible sign that you have been scared. You tend

Nervous systems control fight/flight response

I am going to use an analogy of a racehorse starting a race to describe the two nervous systems involved in the response to threats, composed of the sympathetic nervous system and the parasympathetic nervous system. The sympathetic nervous system is in charge of fight or flight, whilst in opposition the parasympathetic system calms, known as the rest and digest response.

Imagine the horse being let out of the gate at the racetrack; this is the sympathetic nervous system, as the horse takes flight this literally is the fight/flight response. The parasympathetic nervous system is analogous to the jockey; slowing the horse down and restoring the system to balance. Once the horse has left the gate there is pretty much no turning back. Such is the sympathetic nervous system, all or nothing. Panic attacks involve many symptoms and this is the result of all the systems responding to the perceived threat.

The thalamus and hypothalamus of the brain inform the adrenal glands to release two chemicals, adrenaline and noradrenaline, which initiate the fight/flight response. The sympathetic nervous system begins, continues and increases its effects. The body does have many ways to restore equilibrium. However it takes time to wash away these chemicals and for the jockey to slow the horse down. The chemicals are released, and ensure that the anxiety response continues even after the threat has gone or you have decided it is a false alarm. Adrenaline and noradrenaline are chemicals and are reabsorbed and reused by the body. However, this process takes time. While this reabsorption process is happening, you remain in an anxious state. Although it is uncomfortable, it is not going to harm you.

to breathe more rapidly and in order to do that, take more shallow breaths.

Activation of the fight/flight response produces other symptoms like your pupils dilating, increased sweating and a "dry" mouth, nausea and tense muscles. Tension in your neck can result in head-ache and other types of pain. Again there are useful reasons for these symptoms. Sweating allows the body to regulate its tem-perature. Taking in as much light as possible when your pupils are dilated means quite literally you are more vigilant. Tense muscles indicate you are ready to pounce which may be required when facing a significant demand.

The fight/flight response takes a great deal of energy, which makes you feel tired, drained and fatigued – wanting to just return to bed. All of your biological and chemical systems have been activated to deal with a threat and your body often leaves nothing in the tank meaning it makes sense that you are tired.

Your thoughts are critical to kick starting anxiety

Anxiety is a state where you are unable to adapt appropriately to stress in your life. In anxiety those physical symptoms described interact with your thoughts to misattribute the cause of the problem, away from understanding this is a normal physiological response, to a more serious thought. People imagine the worst: for example, for people in an anxious state, dizziness may mean to them that they are about to pass out or numbness may mean they are having a heart attack. Such simple sensations can lead to panic, and panic leads you to making poor decisions or a sense of intense embarrassment. Panic attacks are sudden and intense feelings of fear and physical sensations of your heart racing and breathing becoming shallower. The perception of a threat seems real but there is usually no actual threat. Panic attacks occur when there exist unexpected physical symptoms; a person experiencing panic may have a belief that there will be the worst possible outcome and they respond with panic or fear or both. Because the body is constantly changing and adjusting to changes in the broader environment, there are plenty of opportunities for this misattribution to occur.

Memory is one of the first things that people describe losing when they are distressed. Being easily distracted means you cannot engage in the thorough search you are able to achieve when relaxed. When faced with a threat, humans don't need to be able to remember facts that are not important, such as the name of that beach you visited when you were a child; instead you need to focus on the here and now. When an obvious stressor cannot be found, misattribution is the next critical phase in the stress response.

Memory issues can lead to panic attacks. In very simple terms, the thinking goes along these lines: there is nothing out there that is causing the stress response so there must be a medical problem I don't know about yet. The brain, using the linkages between a hypothesis and looking for evidence to support the initial belief, now searches for and usually finds evidence to lead to an outcome. These perceived, but erroneous, outcomes can be serious such as "I think I am dying", "I am 'losing my mind'", or "I am unable to cope".

Anxiety is concerned with perceptions of the future. It makes you feel that you are vulnerable, the world seems threatening and the future feels unpredictable. You hear it in the questions where people start with "What if . . .?" Do you use this sort of start to a question? Your goal is to move from a question to a statement. Dupont and co-authors, in a book in 2003, described the change that needs to be made to a statement of "So what if . . ." This is hard though, given the strength of the stress response and the distress you may be experiencing.

Anxiety and your interpretation of risk

As mentioned earlier, knowledge is power. The information given to you so far in this chapter about the stress response and anxiety will hopefully help in managing your distress. Anxiety is unpleasant, but it is not dangerous. How we perceive risk and risk assessment is a very important part of anxiety management. Risk is the possibility of something happening, of a future event, and usually refers to a negative impact. Of course, if you buy a lottery ticket you will have a risk of becoming a millionaire. This embeds risk as a future event, something that you can avoid given a suitable intervention. In the lottery example, avoiding having to spend all that prize money by not buying a lottery ticket will reduce the risk of winning the money.

Scientists, doctors and politicians often try to talk to the public so they understand risk. For example, doctors wish us to understand the chances of becoming ill from smoking, or if we miss a vaccination, the risk of getting measles. We now rely on scientific measurement of risk. These use numbers and statistics, and provide a robust estimate of the true risk. However, this is a number, and does not necessarily help in our decision making, particularly as most risks are tiny.

The concept of risk is difficult for humans to assess. By its very nature, considering risk implies that there are at least two options, and the risk varies between the two options. Graham, in the following box, explains some of the scientific understanding of risk.

Stress and risk of poor health

Scientists define risk as between 0%, where there is no risk and the event will not happen, up to 100% where the event is certain to occur. It is rare for a risk of some event to really be as low as 0% or as high as 100%. Human assessment of risk and applying these numbers to our personal situation is far more complex, and open to a large amount of error. These assessments are affected by anxiety; anxiety and risk assessment have been shown to be linked so that you are more likely to be pessimistic about the likelihood of an event when fearful when compared to experiencing another emotion like anger.

Human assessment of risk relies on using qualitative expressions, such as "probably", "likely", or "unlikely". If you ask people to rate the level of probability, between 0% and 100%, for these words you will get a huge difference between people. The subsequent decision making can even be influenced by the way the question is framed. When the risk is given as a positive, such as the risk of living when undergoing surgery, it is more likely to be chosen compared to the negative aspect of exactly the same data.

In scientific studies, stressful life events have been associated with the development of cancer. But of course, just because something is associated does not mean it is a direct cause. The National Cancer Institute in the USA is content that stress is not a direct cause of cancer. There is limited evidence that has shown some weak links, but expert opinion says there is no cause for concern. This is not the same for the impact stress has on health; as a person's ability to cope reduces there is a deterioration in health. A patient's cognitions, their attention, memory and processing of information, and their underlying beliefs regulate their ability to cope with a given situation.

Even when you can successfully identify the risk associated with a stressful event, you must also apply sense to whether you can influence the event or not. For example, you have no control over whether it rains when planning a barbecue.

I hear beliefs of individuals I have treated that are based in anxiety, highlighting the poor assessment of risk. For example, people equate things that they have not experienced with danger. I also hear people assuming the worst will happen, and prepare for this by worrying.

Your mind influences your distress

Cox and McKay, in a paper published in 1978, highlighted the influence your mind has on determining the level of stress you experience. When you think about a situation, imbalance or distress results when your perceived capability does not meet, or is outweighed by, the perceived demand. Imagine a see-saw with the demand at one end and you at the other. Your perception of the situation here is key; having a clear view of what is at the other end, the demand, makes a difference.

You might think that the task is too big or complex, but when you find out more about it, you will identify that it is made up of a series of small tasks; this discovery may also occur when you investigate your strengths. The actual demands, and your strengths or capabilities to deal with the demand, are only discovered by experimenting with the stressor itself, trying to press down on the see-saw from your side. Genetics, early experiences, and personality all play a role here but from a self-help viewpoint, looking at issues around stress is a great place to start and actively explore your world.

A person's ideas, attitudes, and expectations about the world, themselves and their future can mediate the effects of any given stressor. It is proposed that any given stressor is neither good nor bad, but it is the belief a person holds which determines the emotional valency, or our attraction or aversion to an event. For a patient diagnosed with cancer, the implications of a "negative" perception can be important. It has been called "The Big C", a demonstration of the fear that people hold of cancer. If the patient believes there is no hope of survival after cancer, that their entire life no longer holds pleasure and they are powerless to alter the course of their illness, the patient's ability to cope is markedly compromised. If an individual holds these beliefs and exists within a social environment characterized by inadequate support, experiences rigid social boundaries and a limited social role, the patient is likely to have poor health outcomes. Not only could the patient be less likely to engage in behaviours to alter the course of their condition, such as adhering to their medication, they may even actively avoid treatment, believing there is no hope anyway. Not surprisingly, a patient with cancer who refuses treatment is more likely to die than other patients.

Coping techniques can alleviate distress

There are many techniques you could employ. We will give an overview of a number of them, so you can decide which ones you want to try. Don't worry if some of them don't appeal to you or don't work for you. Indeed you could change your thought from "What if this doesn't work?" to "So what if this doesn't work".

Coping technique – Body scan

As previously mentioned, the first coping technique to help alleviate distress is to become more aware of your own body. Start with a mental scan of your entire body beginning at your toes and highlight any areas of your body that are holding tension or that you notice are agitated. This returns to the frog in a boiling pot, to remind you to be aware of distress creeping up on you. Remember, anxiety goes away eventually and it won't do you any harm.

Coping technique – Exposure

A second technique, to break a pattern of trying to cope by avoiding stressful situations, is exposure exercises. Start with a list of ten social situations that are associated with you becoming more stressed. The more you avoid a trigger to your distress, the greater its impact and subsequently the more you believe you need to avoid it next time. Armed with the techniques in this chapter, start at the least distressing item on your list and give yourself a reward when you complete it. By avoidance you also prevent the opportunity of practising your skills, increasing your sensitivity to the thing causing the distress. When you live through the stressful experience, it often isn't as bad as you would have anticipated.

Coping technique – Counterfactuals

A third technique, a cognitive strategy, is to ask whether in a similar world where the cause of your anxiety has been removed, the world would be a better place. This is known as a counterfactual, that is "counter-to-fact". If everything else was the same and the risk factor was removed – would you still be anxious? You may be able to answer the question by looking at people around you – are they behaving scared?

Reassurance seeking is a damaging extension of this technique. When you are distressed, do you ask others for confirmation that there is nothing wrong? As we saw in Chapter 1 "How are you?", there is no good that can come from this. A dependency cycle ensues and the person needs more and more reassurance. Ask the question, would a person without anxiety seek answers to these questions from others?

Coping technique – Listing your strengths

You can defeat dependency by listing your own strengths using the fourth technique. You can defeat the oppressive feelings of anxiety by acknowledging you are not the only person who deals with these sensations. You can counter the need for conformity by eliminating comparison with others and imagining yourself in 20 years' time and asking the question "Will I be concerned about this?" You can experience the emptiness you feel fully without attempting to avoid it and then ask "what now?" If you still struggle with meaninglessness, ask the question again after you have helped another person.

Coping technique – Break it down

Previously we introduced a see-saw analogy to look at the perceived demands and your ability to cope. Breaking tasks down can make demands more manageable and reduce the imbalance causing distress. This is the fifth technique. For example, booking a family holiday may seem too stressful but each smaller element such as booking a flight is more easily achieved. The idea here is to have realistic goals for a situation. Often when you experience distress, you focus on the unrealistic goals you have set for yourself, the anxiety itself, and the negative aspects to you as a person. By having attainable goals, checking in with others about their expectations, focusing on the things that are going right like a calming sensation you feel or your strengths in being able to make it as far as you have, you can start to experiment more and challenge your long held beliefs. Looking back you see that there are things to be learnt from all situations and even hope for the future that you can behave however you see fit, not as dictated by your anxiety.

Coping technique – 10, 9, 8 . . .

Technique number six relates to the fight/flight response, which is a preparation for action, and conversely the aggression experienced by a person can often be put down to them becoming irritated by other people and their lack of action. A simple example is a person who wants to leave a shopping centre and may experience panic. That person may say "why can't people just get out of my way? Can't they see I am in trouble here?" You can use problem-solving skills to deal with this; ask yourself "have I dealt with something similar, or worse, before?" Is this experience the worst thing you have ever endured (10/10) or is it indeed more manageable and not so extreme? Often by doing this you unlock both the strengths you have in stopping it from being the worst and a roadmap for the future on how to improve your mood, getting that 10 down to a 1.

Coping technique – Distraction

Using distraction can be a powerful tool, and this is the seventh technique. People with Social Anxiety Disorder experience an irrational fear of being negatively criticized by others and embarrassing themselves by their own behaviour in a social situation. When distracted, people with SAD report less anxiety and fewer negative beliefs.

Other techniques will also alleviate distress

The fight/flight response also activates the mind in certain ways. You begin to notice the number and speed of your thoughts increase markedly, and this is a response to prepare you for any threats you may encounter, even if they are not apparent yet. Contrast this with "being in the moment", where you have focused attention and heightened concentration. Distress leaves you with thoughts that are everywhere and nowhere simultaneously as you search for possible threats, but do a bad job at thinking clearly about any one thing in particular. Over time you can develop beliefs about yourself that match these thoughts. Relaxation, breathing exercises, and mindfulness are useful techniques to calm an overactive mind, and these are discussed in Chapter 10 "Relaxation techniques". Sleep problems are often a good indicator of stress issues. This may sound strange but only to those people that haven't spent seemingly endless nights worrying and tossing and turning in bed and not sleeping.

Sleep hygiene methods look to associate the act of going to bed with sleeping, which will be covered in detail in Chapter 9 "Leading a balanced lifestyle".

Stress is an essential and natural part of all of us. The more we avoid the triggers, thoughts, and feelings associated with distress, the worse it becomes. Our aim is to accept and manage stress, approach the very things that scare us the most, and adopt the curious mind of a beginner, practising our self-management skills and encouraging our progress. By our knowledge and ability to name the feelings and sensations of a stress response, we can be increasingly optimistic about our ability to prepare, cope, and cherish our successes.

"Post-it" note technique

When you overestimate the risk of failure, you foster beliefs that maintain avoidance and limit the experiences you have. Experiment with this by noting the difference between your expectations and observations. Think of something that you avoid doing or try to avoid, and on a "post-it" note write down what the event is, and rate from 1 to 10 how distressing it is. Challenge yourself to do that and afterwards rate how distressing it actually was.

You could start with something small, such as saying "hello" to someone, maybe someone you don't know. Then you could use further "post-it" notes when you increase the level of challenge. At the end of each day, record any events that occurred, how you felt, and any other observations. Compare your expectations already written down with your observations during the week.

By challenging your long held beliefs about what you expect to happen, you are able to change your thinking to make it more realistic, taking into account all your past experiences, alternative explanations, and the common sense you have.

Chapter 6

UNHAPPINESS

Danielle watched on the sidelines as her life fell apart. At 27, like 1 in 4 people living in the UK with a mental health problem, she was struggling; living at home with her parents, she had dropped out of university and even found the thought of looking for a job just too overwhelming. Sitting in front of me she said "I see people on a different plane. I am just wallowing in the mud feeling hopeless. I just don't know what to do. If I take baby steps and hit a stumbling block then it sort of sends me off in that direction [as she points down]. If I try, I might fail and if I fail then that is bad. That's how my brain works." I asked her "What about when you succeed?" and with a flat and resigned response she said it is "Fairly rare but if I do succeed then I don't feel proud of myself. I think, other people can do this why should I be happy with myself. I know it is a bad way to live. This is built-in pessimism."

Unhappiness or low mood is becoming one of the most significant burdens we face as individual people, and society as a whole. This is mainly due to the way these problems influence our thinking, and how they can make us feel undesirable, defective, and worthless. Unhappiness does not have to reflect some sort of psychological problem but can be a normal reaction to events in your life. Low mood and unhappiness are components of the medical disorder known as "Major Depressive Disorder": commonly known as "depression" or sometimes referred to as "clinical depression".

Rest assured, this is not a new phenomenon, as depressive illness was recognized in ancient Greece in the time of Hippocrates, over two thousand years ago. Low mood may be brought on by a major life event such as death of a close family member. But many people suffer from unhappiness without such a trigger in their lives. Throughout this chapter we will use the scientific and clinical advances made in the field of depression treatment to help deal with problems associated with unhappiness.

But why do I feel this way?

Common situations and patterns can be found, preceding the development of an episode of low mood, or even depression. Chronic illness, the experience of pain, or stressful life events can lead a person down the path to low mood. These can then, if you are unable to successfully deal with them, lead to an episode of depression. For example, when any person experiences a relationship breakdown they have a period where they don't enjoy the things they used to enjoy; they end up feeling bad. Normally after a period of time the person starts socializing, having a good time again, and recovering their previous patterns in life. Those that don't may be on the road to depression.

You may ask yourself when you are down: "what is the cause of my mood?" There is seldom a single cause of ongoing problems with low mood, so from the outset this is a complex issue. There is evidence that some people with depression come from families that have struggled with mental health problems as well. Your risk of depression is higher if your parents or a brother or sister has a problem managing their mood. Notice I am talking here about risk and not the cause: just because a family member has this problem does not mean this has caused depression in you. This is important and links back to our discussion in Chapter 2 "Challenge your thinking".

When I look at the research on stressful life events, which mainly lie outside the person's control, the evidence is strong linking these life events to depression. Depression is associated with serious events such as job loss, widowhood, or divorce. Negative major life events are associated with depression and the presence of the disorder can elicit or exacerbate these events. The evidence to propose this as a cause has not been collected. As discussed in Chapter 2 "Challenge your thinking", a randomized controlled trial would provide best evidence of this. However it would be impractical, if not impossible, to do such a trial – how would you "give" someone a major negative life event to see if it leads to low mood?

It seems likely that the brain reacts to these events in some sort of biological sense. However, members of the medical community don't agree on the role played by problems with neurotransmitters and other biological problems in depression. We do know that anti-depressant medications, which act on these neurotransmitters directly, are often effective treatments.

Descriptive words are important

Eskimos are said to have many words for the concept of snow which includes subtleties like snow particles, formations, and

---

Unhappiness – what does it mean?

abandoned, alone, anguished, awful, betrayed, blue, burdened, cheated, damaged, defeated, deflated, dejected, depressed, deprived, deserted, despondent, devalued, diminished, disappointed, discontented, disheartened, down, downcast, dreadful, empty, excluded, forgotten, forlorn, friendless, frustrated, gloomy, heavy-hearted, helpless, humiliated, ignored, inadequate, incapable, incompetent, inept, inferior, insulted, intimidated, isolated, jilted, let-down, lonely, lost, low, mediocre, melancholy, miserable, moody, neglected, oppressed, pained, pathetic, persecuted, powerless, put-down, rejected, rotten, sad, scorned, slighted, snubbed, sorrowful, terrible, troubled, uncomfortable, unhappy, unworthy, upset, useless, weary, worried.

fallen snow. In our language there is an extraordinary range of words we use to describe feelings of unhappiness. Take a look through the words in the box on the previous page, which are just a sample of these words. Do you use any of them when describing yourself? Does anyone else remark on you using these descriptive words?

If someone asks you how you are, what do you say in response? People will often say they are "fine". Other offenders include "being OK". Both of these are examples of a catch-all that can be used when people don't pinpoint how they really feel. What you should aim for instead is to be more specific in describing your mood and therefore making it more manageable, which will help with your confidence in dealing with your unhappiness.

Other ways to describe feeling bad or low

Words for feeling blue are to be found below, how many can you find?

d	d	e	j	e	c	t	e	d	s	n	s	h
e	e	o	m	e	l	d	e	b	a	s	e	d
s	s	e	n	d	e	h	c	t	e	r	w	w
p	s	g	l	o	o	m	i	n	e	s	s	o
o	e	l	h	w	d	a	l	f	l	d	n	l
n	r	o	o	n	c	u	o	n	l	c	b	l
d	p	o	p	w	f	h	h	u	u	a	i	o
e	e	m	e	e	d	s	c	h	d	s	t	h
n	d	y	l	g	h	u	n	h	a	p	p	y
c	r	o	e	e	l	b	a	r	e	s	i	m
y	d	s	s	e	l	p	l	e	h	u	d	e
k	c	i	s	t	r	a	e	h	d	h	l	c
y	a	h	l	g	l	p	m	s	t	u	s	b

Improving your mood means getting to grips with the language of mood. The puzzle on the previous page will help with this task. By using more specific language to identify your mood, not only can you breakdown a nebulous cloud of mood into smaller and more manageable bits of information, you are less likely to generalize and this tendency is important in talking about the thoughts associated with depression.

Behavioural symptoms may define your unhappiness

The main behavioural symptoms of depression are avoidance, ineffectual coping, and poor social skills. Avoidance and ineffectual coping interact with each other so that the more you avoid a perceived stressful situation, the less practice you get at coping with it; the skills you may once have had wither and die. This affects how you feel and can reinforce your unhelpful beliefs.

Unhappiness and depression in social settings can be problematic. A fairly modern phenomenon is how people can be obsessed with their mobile phones. They sit with their phone on their laps all of the time, they glance at the screen, and do not engage with others in their company as they are distracted by the texts or Facebook entries on their device. These poor social skills can be a sign of underlying unhappiness.

There are various strategies you may wish to use to deal with avoidance symptoms, such as graded exposure described in Chapter 4 "Self-efficacy". You may also try the "five-minute attempt" which is a useful way to test out your beliefs, as well as helping you to notice the motivation you can build through attempting an activity. The idea behind five-minute attempts is to give yourself five minutes to deal with a task and know that you are able to stop after this period has elapsed. Often the problem of avoidance is compounded through lack of motivation. People often say "I will start it when I feel motivated". What happens if that motivation never appears? What about the motivation you build while doing an activity? By experimenting with five-minute attempts at a task, you can manage avoidance, build confidence, and see your achievements.

As an example, if you are struggling with a specific piece of work and keep putting it to the bottom of the pile of things to deal with, perhaps you could try the five-minute attempt. Tell yourself you are just going to spend five minutes working on it. How does this make you feel? You will be able to put it to one side in five minutes' time. Is this a useful exercise? Did you feel less pressure when you knew you only had to spend five minutes? Did this build your motivation to continue? Did you in fact get it all completed much more easily than you thought you would?

Unhappiness causes physiological symptoms

There is a range of physiological symptoms that accompany unhappiness or low mood: these can be severe and debilitating in extreme cases. Physiological symptoms include sleep disturbances, appetite disturbance, and decreased sexual interest. Sleep problems can be both a lack of good quality sleep, or excessive sleep particularly in the daytime. Insomnia where you cannot get back to sleep after waking early is a common complaint. Excessive eating may also be a symptom, or loss of appetite. Both of these can reduce energy levels and make life seem even more difficult.

Looking at the myriad of physical symptoms of depression introduces us to one of many coping strategies: measurement of how we feel in a physiological sense. This may relate to sleep quality, appetite, or feelings of pain.

An exercise to try is to assess a typical week and look at the times when you feel as though you achieve things, and also when you don't. Measure the times you feel pleasure, or unhappiness by briefly recording your week on paper. Notice when you sleep well, eat well, and generally feel happy and the times when you feel the opposite. You usually discover how quickly your mood changes and how normal this is. You will also see exactly where you get your happiness from and what opportunities there are to improve on this.

Mood-related symptoms are common in unhappiness

The different emotions that you may be aware of experiencing, whilst having a low mood, cover many different areas. You may feel anger, which we have dealt with in Chapter 3 "Anger". Guilt is a common feeling too when unhappy, where you feel that some of your behaviour or outcomes from something you have been part of, violates the moral compass that helps guide you. Taking this further, you may also feel remorse for the things you feel guilty over, that loss of an alternate outcome if you had behaved differently.

A closely related mood is shame, which is difficult to disentangle from guilt and embarrassment. It seems that whilst guilt is about a violation of your own personal value system, shame applies to other people's values or society's. This fits with the modern thinking that the word derives from a word describing the act of covering oneself up. This is what you wish to do when you feel shame.

Sadness is commonly confused with depression, and they are closely linked. We all have different skills at dealing with our own sadness, and sadness in other people. Some people are gifted at using humour, others may use distraction as a coping mechanism. Anxiety is a common mood for people, and this is closely aligned with low mood, unhappiness, and depression. I have dealt with this in Chapter 5 "Distress".

A person's self-esteem, and their belief that they can change things for the better, are affected directly by life events; for example a relationship breakdown is an experience that may be outside the person's control. This leaves the person with the belief that it is their fault, it will be like this forever and there is nothing good in their world.

Unhappiness affects your thoughts or cognitive symptoms

When you feel low this affects the way you think as we discussed in Chapter 2 "Challenge your thinking", and this results in some of the cognitive symptoms of depression. You may feel indecisiveness, where you are unable to make a firm decision. Why does this happen? Sometimes you are right to delay making a decision until you have generated sufficient evidence to support your plans. But you may find that indecision is crippling your life and in very serious circumstances this is known as aboulomania. You may want to experiment further with the five-minute attempts, to see how making a decision affects you. You may feel overwhelmed, unable to deal with situations coming your way. This is where taking small steps, bite-sized chunks, is a good approach to tackling this symptom.

Concentration can feel hampered, and this is a negative cycle as poor concentration may lead you to not successfully completing a task. This may lead to further feelings of unhappiness and further loss of concentration. This may come about, in part, due to problems with sleep and appetite. Relaxation and other techniques may help to relieve this symptom.

The power of thoughts which fit into your beliefs

Beliefs are the changeable core of us as humans. Beliefs help you to interpret events and make decisions quickly. By allowing you to quickly decide whether an event is going to be good or bad, safe or threatening, painful or pleasurable, you can avoid negative outcomes. You are more likely to survive because your beliefs apply these quick and dirty labels. You can also use beliefs to attempt to predict future events. One problem is that you rarely go back and work out when these beliefs have been accurate and indeed when they were just plain wrong.

Beliefs form a centre that helps you feel grounded. Like an anchor, you can attach yourself to who you believe you are, your identity, and help get a clearer idea of your strengths and weaknesses. Beliefs are both the description of you and the structure itself. You have beliefs about your worth, your future, and your world. Beliefs are *the* important determinant of how you feel. These feelings can be strong and when this is the case, can determine what you decide to do or not to do.

Beliefs are expressed in your thoughts, feelings, and actions. Your thoughts are the accessible components of some of your deepest and most inaccessible beliefs. These beliefs are just ideas you think are true, often without testing to see if they are. Familiar situations often trigger automatic thoughts that are simply generalized responses.

If you have a belief that states that you are incompetent, you will avoid situations or activities which require you to show competency. If this continues, you don't try new things, you miss opportunities and narrow the scope of interactions in your world. Sometimes the anchor of your negative, restrictive beliefs is set so deep that you can hardly see it, or know how it started. Your consciousness is layered in this way such that some thoughts are easily accessible and you can expose them to the light of scrutiny easily. Others are hidden away and difficult to get at.

Irrespective of this, you get upset at yourself when you fail to live up to these beliefs. The more you apply these beliefs, the more automatic they become and the rules which govern them are set deeper and deeper in your consciousness, sometimes below conscious awareness. Furthermore you may act on a belief without thinking about what the belief actually means.

For example: thoughts like "I can't handle this, it is beyond my abilities, I will probably screw this up, what is the point in trying, nothing I do works anyway!" As a result of these negative automatic thoughts, you put minimal effort into the task, spend a lot of time thinking about these thoughts or procrastinating and become more frustrated and finally give up, often before you have actually begun.

When a child is bullied, abused, or set unrelenting standards, they tend to believe the negative messages they are exposed to, and store them as beliefs. Beliefs are often formed in childhood and continue to develop throughout our adolescent and adult lives. Families and friends influence the development of beliefs which we often adopt without questioning, particularly the beliefs that were dominant within our families. These can be in the form of sayings and if they are repeated often enough, they sink deeper into our psyche and beyond our awareness.

Negative beliefs often lead to the practice of failure

A self-defeating belief is a good example of a negative belief. A negative belief involves a way of thinking which makes it less likely that you will achieve your goals: "I hope I don't mess up when I go to work today." Negative beliefs and thoughts are an aspect of depression. If you think negatively, you will feel negative, which will increase the likelihood of failure in what you are doing. For example, when you constantly rehearse to yourself that you must not forget the milk on the way home from work this leads to other things that you have forgotten. Then you may get distracted and walk right past the store. What causes you to bring home some milk is actually buying the milk, not spending all day worrying about it. That worry though, in itself, distracts you.

Here are some examples of negative beliefs: "I am not good enough"; "I need to be in a relationship to be happy"; "Life is full of dangers"; "Other people are selfish and ruthless"; "I have to do things perfectly to be worthwhile."

We also add some overestimation to this mix. Shavitt et al. (1999) identified that we all tend to overestimate how often we are right. Beliefs are adaptive and helpful when our beliefs are accurate. A belief about your vulnerability in dark places helps you to make decisions about areas to avoid, which protects your safety. However your belief that you are incompetent has only a small basis of truth, but has enormous implications and a cascading effect. This belief might lead you to avoid all new challenges, resulting in doubts about your abilities which results in low self-esteem, unassertive behaviour, and stagnation in your life. But how does the brain work like this? Graham explains some modern thinking about how our brains work in the following box.

Two systems for thinking

Kahneman in his recent book *Thinking, Fast and Slow* dismissed the idea that people are generally rational. He spent his pre-Nobel prize winning years identifying errors in thinking. He identified two systems at work in the mind from these decades of research. They are not parts of the brain that may be seen using a scanner, but scientific constructions that may help to explain how the mind works. System 1 uses association and images or metaphors to produce a rough guide of reality, whilst system 2 draws on explicit beliefs and reason to make choices.

System 1 is said to "propose", while system 2 "disposes". System 2 often accepts the easy but unreliable guide about the world that system 1 delivers. System 1 delivers an intuitive conclusion based on a "heuristic" – an easy but risky way of answering questions – and system 2 believes this answer without bothering to ask any questions.

People might want to employ reasoning to improve their thoughts. Words themselves can communicate our thoughts but they can also get us into trouble as Koestler notes in his book, *The Act of Creation*. He quotes LL White in saying "reason as we know it, is never aware of its hidden assumptions". The words we use are the best we have at the time but are they the best for labelling our thoughts, describing our feelings, and then providing the basis for the logic arguments for guiding our actions? Eureka moments in science are seldom the result of directed logical argument but come seemingly out of nowhere or indeed as Archimedes found, in the bath. To invent, Souriau noted, "you must put thought aside".

w let's take it a step further. Reanney in 1994 wrote about quantum waves as "not existing in the time and space of ordinary experience, it encodes information, if you focus on one aspect, other aspects become fuzzy, it only becomes 'real' when you look at it". And he notes how similar this is to the idea of having thoughts. Thoughts cannot be measured in time, they are packed with information and when you focus on one, others are temporarily lost. A thought is "real" when seen in the "mind's eye" which is the ability to construct and generate an image with your mind.

Three common negative beliefs in people with low mood

There are three beliefs or types of thinking that are commonly found in people with low mood or depression. They relate to the past, future, and you as a person:

1. A negative view of yourself. When you feel low it is easier to be critical of your achievements and you as a person. Often this comes from setting too high a standard and unrealistic goals for perfection. These expectations are impossible to consistently live up to and therefore the belief that the problem lies within you internally develops.
2. A negative view of your past. When you feel low, it is as if your vision is narrow and you pay attention only to the negative events of your life. This process results in a biased view of your past life.
3. A negative view of your future. When you are low, you are more likely to predict doom and gloom. This expectation of unpleasant experiences adds to a sense of helplessness and lack of control. As a result you often avoid experiences that are the very things that challenge this view and provide some positive aspects to life.

"Post-it" note technique

It has been said that we can see the same thing in one of three ways; as negative, neutral, or from a positive perspective. For example, your weight and body can be seen in these three ways. You may feel neutral towards your weight, or maybe in a negative way such that you feel you want to lose or gain weight. Alternatively, you may feel very positively about your body.

Write down a topic you would like to think more positively about, for example your job, or a member of your family. List as many things as possible that are positive or interesting about the topic, with at least five entries. Thinking about the positive aspects is unlikely to happen all by itself so use the "Premack principle". This is where you can do something that you would not normally do frequently, by tying it to something that you do frequently. So, you could choose something you do lots of times per day, such as taking a drink or using your phone. Then before you do it, think about the positive list and repeat in your mind to yourself one of the entries on the list. After a week, ask yourself how you feel about your topic.

People with mood problems are able to internalize and take responsibility for negative things that happen to them easily. However, this personal agency, taking responsibility for starting and completing one's actions, is lacking when it comes to positive things that happen to them. In a meta-analysis of 104 studies on attributional style in people with depression, Sweeney et al. in

1986 described finding that when things go bad, attributions to internal, stable, and global causes were associated with depression. When things go well, attributions to external, unstable, and specific causes were also associated with depression. This happens when the good or bad thing is real or imagined or when it occurs to different people suffering depression. In short, when bad things happen the mud this produces sticks, whilst in contrast the good stuff is like Teflon and slides right off. Self-serving bias and confirmation bias both have a role to play here, both of which were covered earlier in Chapter 2 "Challenge your thinking".

But how do we fix this? Given that your confidence in your reasoning and decision making is biased by attempts to justify your answer you selectively focus on evidence supporting your answer and disregarding evidence against it. When you think of reason-based choice you might think you are doing the best you can but you might actually be shifting the focus from the outcomes or options to a focus on choosing the best reasons to support your choice. Choices based on reasons are reinforced when people have to justify themselves, perceived as easier to justify and less likely to be criticized, and give rise to more elaborate explanations.

What keeps unhelpful beliefs going?

So what do you do? Koestler in 1971 suggested abdicating and promoting. Abdication is the giving up of power; you chase that power through a belief that you must be in control of your thoughts at all times. Routines and rules which govern your thoughts are removed and you can then become more creative in your thinking. Removing this promotes more basic thoughts and indeed allows true feelings to surface. Intuition gets a bigger say or is promoted.

When you try to develop new ideas that will someday blossom into a new belief system, your mind reacts. A new idea can represent disruption to the status quo, and as a consequence change is considered to be bad. What you seldom do is identify the evidence against this new idea being something you should react against. Rarely do you list the costs associated with maintaining the status quo or indeed list the advantages of change.

Often when I ask a person how they feel about something, they will try to convince me of the correctness of the reasons for their beliefs. Coming from a perspective that is non-judgemental, it leaves me curious as to what leads a person to go into quite excessive detail at this point. A series of questions emerge. Who are you trying to convince? Why are you trying to convince me? What if you were on a desert island, would there be a need to talk about this in this way?

Once you have a negative belief in your mind, there is a tendency to then interpret new information and selectively identify data that matches this belief. This is known as confirmation bias, again referring you back to Chapter 2 "Challenge your thinking". Researchers have collected evidence across science, medicine, and the law that supports the premise that confirmation bias is alive and well irrespective of cognitive ability; so just because you're clever it doesn't mean that you're immune from confirmation bias. People rarely seek evidence that would show a hypothesis to be wrong even though you understand that this is an effective strategy to show it to be correct – if it indeed is so. Some brain imaging research suggests that consistent data, linking to a causal theory, recruits neural tissue in a different area of the brain when evaluating inconsistent data.

You can get over confirmation bias by actively seeking out counterexamples and becoming a sleuth to find evidence that contradicts your viewpoint. This bias also might work in elections where a citizen will stick to their original beliefs about a party or candidate as they believe that other citizens, having lived a life similar to them, would vote in the same manner. A "rational" thought that supports their original belief in the candidate, but also doesn't include looking for any alternate evidence.

Aim to change your negative thoughts to more realistic thoughts

People can often make their condition worse and even bring on low moods by the manner in which they think. It is important to become aware of the negative ways in which you may think and learn to change these in order to stop yourself adding to your woes. The way you think often controls how you feel. It can therefore make you anxious or calm, sad or content. Recognition of these thoughts is the key. You must learn to recognize your own negative thoughts, and then learn how to change them into positive thoughts. This helps to plan for your successes, not your failures. When an Olympic athlete imagines their race before the starting gun, they see themselves flying over every hurdle, not crashing at the first obstacle.

When setting goals, aim to identify things that you would be doing more of to tell you that things were working out better. It is easy to walk into your bedroom and see that someone has left a towel on the bed. However, what is more difficult is to walk into the bedroom and tell an observer that there was a towel on the bed and now it is gone. We can do this with our goals. What will you be doing more of when you reach your goal? What will you see and how will it feel?

"Post-it" note technique

Now write a gratitude journal one day at a time on a "post-it" note. By noticing kindness, this helps you become able to identify when this occurs in your day and even change your day because of it. Each day for the next two weeks, write down three things that you feel gratitude about. These could be small things like the sun shining on a morning or bigger things like your health or a message you receive from a friend.

In the second week, start another "post-it" note and identify the causes of each of these things you feel gratitude about. Consider how much of the stuff you feel good about is under your control and how much is outside of it. The results will surprise you.

Chapter 7

WELL-BEING AND HAPPINESS

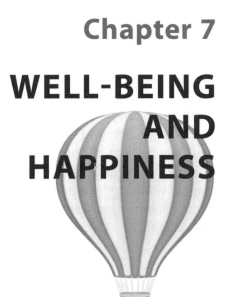

I was talking with Margaret, a middle-aged woman who worked in the local primary school. She said to me: "I just want to feel happy. I used to be a happy go lucky kind of person but don't seem to be able to feel like that anymore." I asked her what she meant by happy. What would need to change in her life for her to feel happy. Her only response was a shrug of her shoulders.

Do I need to define happiness? I know this sounds odd, but we all have an intuitive understanding of what we mean by the word. It is a much-used word, describing a state of positive emotions – it is a good place to be. I am sure you know about the emoticon "smiley", three characters ":-)" that millions of us put in our texts or emails to friends, family, and colleagues. This represents happiness, a physical manifestation of the emotion. But is happiness all we are striving to attain? Happiness is notoriously difficult to pin down, and it's difficult to work out how to improve it for ourselves.

There is a growing understanding of the importance of well-being, which can seem to be beyond happiness and is linked with health and society in many different ways. Aboriginal Australians incorporate community health and spiritual well-being as core aspects of their definition of health. In Western societies, Bircher in 2005 noted that health is "a dynamic state of well-being characterized by a physical and mental potential, which satisfies the demands of life commensurate with age, culture, and personal responsibility". You will notice how both of these statements contain the word well-being, but do not define the word. It is as though we should have an intuitive understanding and knowledge of the word. But is this true?

The discovery of the aspects of well-being requires uncovering what has always been there but obscured from view by long-established habits. Gauss said "I have had my solutions for a long time, but I did not yet know how I am to arrive at them" (James 1890).

Research has begun to support the widely held belief that well-being offers protection against cardiovascular problems and premature death. Graham, in the next box, gives you an example of the research and what this means for you. This all seems to agree with Daniel Gilbert who summarized the research on happiness and found that in the majority of cases, money can't buy love or happiness.

Satisfaction with life and health

In the United Kingdom, two very large studies of civil servants were set up to examine the association between health and factors within eight life domains like sex, marital relationships, family life, feelings about themselves as a person and others. Many thousands of men and women were recruited to the study and have been followed for over 50 years to see what happens to them over time. This is known as a cohort study in epidemiology.

One of the outcomes of interest was coronary heart disease (CHD) with events such as angina, non-fatal myocardial infarction (MI) and death from CHD. The four domains job, family life, sex life, and self-satisfaction were independently associated with a 12% reduced risk of CHD. Looking at CHD, risk of angina was reduced among individuals with high and moderate satisfaction, compared with individuals with low satisfaction.

You can think of well-being as the estimation or understanding you have about how you are doing in your life. This is a summary judgement of the quality of your life, comprising of your personal ups and downs and matching what you are doing with what you have achieved compared with your personal goals.

How does well-being fit with medicine? The medical world seems to have a clear understanding of what it takes to deal with things when they don't go well. Emergency rooms are filled with equipment to help put you back together again. Emergency rooms don't exist that treat well-being and happiness. The World Health Organization (the WHO) early in its life in 1946 decided it must define the word "health" as ". . . a state of complete physical, mental and social well-being and not merely the absence of disease or infirmity". This assumes that health is only possible when all is in perfect working order, ignoring that many people deal with chronic lifelong diseases but would still consider themselves healthy. This is particularly obvious as we grow older: at what point do we place less focus on the physical aspect of well-being and yet still feel healthy?

In 2007, the Istanbul Declaration, signed by the United Nations and many other global organizations, affirmed the commitment to working out how to measure and improve well-being. The science that deals with measuring health and ill-health, known as the science of epidemiology, must measure defined entities or things. Graham describes a little more about this in the next box.

The construct of well-being has been the subject of serious study and an American named Martin Seligman has led the way. In his recent book *Flourish*, published in 2012, Seligman has created a system that breaks down positive psychology into five distinct elements. These can be summarized into the acronym PERMA which stands for Positive emotions, Engagement, Relationships, Meaning, and Accomplishment.

Measuring well-being

The simplest way for scientists to measure well-being is to assess the absence of health: illness or disease, falling within the science of epidemiology. This means we do not often measure well-being which is a subtly different construct. Scientists have struggled to measure the construct of well-being as it is, in their terminology, a "latent variable". This means it exists but it is not directly measurable, unlike your height or the number of cigarettes you smoke as you can measure and count these.

Scientists and politicians are however beginning to realize that measuring well-being using health as a basis is not necessarily appropriate. Some large national studies have been set up, for example "Understanding Society" which is a study in the United Kingdom. This study looks to answer questions about health, but also ambitions, trust, feelings of strain, confidence, worthlessness, happiness, and lifestyle. Some of the diverse areas of interest include individual characteristics, local issues, national, and even international events that influence well-being. For example, the global financial problems have had direct effect on people and their feelings of well-being.

"P" is for positive emotions which we all wish to experience

I think you can probably already make a list of some positive emotions, such as pleasure, joy, hope, and pride. These are all mental states that you strive to achieve which involve warmth; that feeling you get when your body is relaxed. One such expression of this is laughter, which is liberation and emotion without thought. We have described in previous chapters how our emotions are often not able to keep pace with reason. Often our emotions become separated from our reasoning and when we laugh we are performing an emotion without any thought. Just as the flight/fight response is initiated long before we realize what made us startled, so too laughter has developed as the product of a million years of evolution. Our conscious mind often lags behind when we try and talk about what makes us laugh in the first place.

Happiness is the expression of pleasure and contentment usually about an experience, and like laughter involves our thoughts, feelings, and actions. As mentioned earlier, happiness is one part of well-being. Murchison, writing in 1930, wrote: "The wisdom which has come to me from . . . achievements finds expression thus: to recognize and accept one's limitations cheerfully, bravely, but also intelligently; to choose as vocation, and to render service through work for which one is well fitted by nature and acquisition, and, in so doing, to utilize one's special abilities to the utmost. This is the best recipe I have discovered for social usefulness and for personal happiness."

As Murchison described so eloquently, happiness is usually present when something you are doing matches the values you have, whether it be work or play. For example, you might feel happy when spending time with your family, if being family-oriented is a strong value of yours. Happiness often occurs when you achieve something that has a positive personal meaning to you.

The varied answers that people give to the question "what makes you happy?" are also indicative of this. Doing something for someone, coming to someone's aid, helping someone with a task is often associated with happiness. We could call it being an "ethical hedonist". Philosophers talk about ethical hedonists as utilitarians in as much as saying not only do these people see happiness as good, but also that it must be with the good for the greatest number in mind. This is the utilitarian component that I described in Chapter 2 "Challenge your thinking". You are doing something that helps the greatest number of people, in this case you and the other person.

Whilst you may interpret this to mean you should look for the most immediate gains in happiness, it would be incorrect. I am not saying that happiness is only a direct consequence of your actions as there may well be happiness in the doing as well as the outcome. The joy of the action itself or the engagement is important.

An "attitude of gratitude", described by Wood and colleagues in 2010, is associated with better health, better sleep, satisfaction with life, kinder behaviour toward others, and less anxiety and depression. Gratitude is more than just feeling good, it helps to enhance empathy, which is the ability to recognize what emotion another person is experiencing. Gratitude is also the emotion of friendship where you raise your estimates of how much value you hold in the eyes of another person. Gratitude is when someone does something that causes you to realize that you matter more than you thought. You may have discovered some of these things when you completed the "gratitude journal" task at the end of the previous chapter.

What does this mean in everyday terms? Gratitude requires saying thank you for every thoughtful gesture or kindness that you notice. This might also take you to express your admiration for someone's skills or talents or even listening to a story patiently. "If you want to sleep more soundly, count blessings, not sheep," Dr Emmons advises in *Thanks!* a recent summary of the research in this area published in 2007.

Martin Seligman has found that writing a 300-word letter to someone who changed your life can significantly improve your mood. In the letter, you need to be specific about what the person did, how you felt, and what it meant to you. An important component of this practice is to deliver and read the letter in person.

"E" is for Engagement in something that gives enjoyment

Engagement involves the experience often cited by Olympic athletes when they are "in the zone". People may talk about a flow experience; feeling at one with something you are engaged in. This can be something in your work, or a hobby or pastime that you devote energy to such as music or dancing.

Engagement tends to be most closely related to artistic projects, but you can feel engaged on almost any project. The process of writing this book for example has required an enormous dedication of time from us, and our families, to engage fully in writing. You will have things that occupy your time that require engagement. Engagement in something considerably improves the success of that activity.

Reducing the distractions will allow you to concentrate more fully, to do better at the activity, and maybe slip into that state of flow that you may strive for. This requires you to be more careful about the way you spend your time and to be more focused on a certain activity. This may be where "multi-tasking" could get in the way of totally focusing on a single activity or goal.

Research by Paul Bloom has found that understanding more about a subject can increase your pleasure in that subject. For example,

knowing more about classical music can improve your apprecia-
tion of classical music. This is closely related to engagement, and
may help you to increase your PERMA.

"R" is for Relationships which are critical to our state of well-being

The third element to well-being is relationships. Social support is
defined as a perception of being loved and valued. In practical
terms it can be seen as the assistance provided to individuals by
members of their relationship network, in dealing with their subjective and objective needs. A large and ever growing amount of
research on social support identifies that it can influence health
and mental health directly and indirectly.

As researchers we have significant experience in cancer diagnosis
and treatment with most people agreeing that cancer is one of the
most significant events in their life. A review of the literature, by
Wortman in 1984, on patients with cancer found that during this
highly stressful experience, the higher a patient's level of social
support, the lower their level of distress. A patient may recruit
people from their social support network during these periods of
high stress and face lesser stresses alone.

How does this help? Social support can be beneficial for people in
two ways. The "direct effect" model of network membership and
social interaction improves adaptive thinking and functional
behaviours. Social support may encourage a person to do the very
things that help them the most. For example, to persevere and
adhere to a healthy diet and take the medication they are pre-
scribed in spite of initial side effects or problems with motivation
to do so. Social support can also help them to manage stress
better, increase self-esteem, and directly improve the person's
ability to cope.

The second benefit of social support is described by the "stress buffering" hypothesis, which proposes that social support reduces the threat of a stressor, and therefore its physical response. As we saw in Chapter 5 "Distress", stress is the mental equation you make in your head when you weigh up the perceived threat versus your perceived capability to deal with the threat. Remember the see-saw analogy?

Hann and colleagues, in 1995, identified particular elements of social support as important for patients with the most difficult stage of a cancer diagnosis, when they have advanced cancer. These included the number of members of the household and the number of confidants the patient had. The perceived adequacy of each type of support and the total amount of social support was associated with lower levels of depression. Poor social functioning was also a significant predictor of depressive symptoms in lung cancer patients up to a year after diagnosis. More generally, unmarried cancer patients experience a poorer treatment response, lower overall survival, and a greater number go untreated.

"M" is for Meaning which gives a larger purpose to life

The fourth element in the PERMA model of well-being is meaning. This relates to the idea that there is a larger purpose to life and attachment to this bigger cause increases well-being. An example would be offering to help give out food to homeless people or running a class at a local school to share your skills as these things involve more than simply thinking about yourself.

The spiritual factors involved in the cancer experience, which are separate from religious institutions and denote a process of transformation, centre around a feeling of "connectedness". These can be explained through a need to make sense of how the world works and more importantly, explanations for when it fails to adhere to a set of beliefs. Spiritual distress can occur when there is dissonance between an experience and belief. For example, when a patient believes positive thinking improves health and is presented with a cancer recurrence, distress can occur because of feelings of failure and also the direct challenge a recurrence represents to the belief. In a small study, Chibnall and colleagues, writing in 2002, found poor spiritual well-being was positively related to higher levels of distress.

When people establish a meaning to a life-threatening disease, the results are not always negative. In a review of the literature in 1998, Kornblith noted the perceived "second chance" at life that patients experience, with some patients reporting lower levels of psychological distress when compared to patients without cancer. Further, this includes a reprioritization of life goals and strengthening of spiritual beliefs that can also occur for a significant minority of people. This chimes with the accounts about people changing their lifestyle and goals when they have experienced their life being under threat.

In summary of some interesting work by Heatherton, stories people use to describe their own successful changes often have meaning at their core. People are more likely to mention intense emotional experiences: re-evaluating goals and life meaning that crystallizes their discontent with how things are, and influences their motivation to change. The motivation people require to change comes from knowledge of an escape from adverse circumstances that are seen as stable, while at the same time re-evaluating the desirability of their life role. Observing something happening to someone else also is more likely to influence the person to change. The research here also found that people who changed were more likely to make a public declaration, telling others the change was meaningful to them.

"A" is for Accomplishment whether it is big or small

The final component of the PERMA approach to well-being is accomplishment. This may be something big, such as doing a sponsored run, or something much smaller, such as meeting someone on time as planned. All of these accomplishments allow you to improve well-being. In a much more profound sense, take a moment to answer the following questions:

● What have you achieved in your life?
● If you were to write your eulogy what would it contain?
● How have you helped your friends?
● How does your resume or CV sound?

These – admittedly rather stark – questions allow you to re-frame your successes in a fairly objective way. An increase in well-being will be achieved, in part, by improving and developing the answers to these questions over time.

Well-being is more than just happiness

This broader concept of well-being can be very helpful when talking about how to improve your happiness. It shows that the pursuit of positive emotions is very important but that this alone is not enough. It becomes easier to understand the benefits of spending time pursuing other aspects of the PERMA model some-times at the expense of pleasure.

For example, you may find yourself caring for a sick or ageing family member. Although this may reduce some of the pleasurable activities in your life, ultimately you may find you have a greater sense of well-being. You may find more meaning in your own life and satisfaction in accomplishing the difficult job of caring. The relationship between you and the person you are caring for may well be strengthened by the experience.

Optimism influences a person's well-being

Leaving behind the PERMA model, we will now describe more about the importance of optimism, mentioned in Chapter 2 "Challenge your thinking". Optimism is characterized by the view of the world where the "glass is half full", as opposed to the pessimist who sees the "glass is half empty". Optimism is the tendency to look on the more favourable or positive side of life, see the good in events or conditions, and expect the most positive outcome. Pessimism is the opposite. Graham describes over the page some of the science linking optimism and health.

What does the research mean in practical terms? Optimism is related to better adjustment and an ability to deal with stress, because of the coping strategies these people use. There are two types of optimism but here we talk about dispositional optimism which is where you expect the best possible outcome from any situation. This form of optimism is positively associated with exposure or active coping strategies. These are the behaviours a person uses to eliminate, reduce, or manage stressors or emotions. On the flip side, optimists are significantly less likely to use avoidance coping strategies. These behaviours seek to ignore, avoid, or withdraw from stressors or emotions. An optimist is also able to deal with failure and disappointment, a key requirement for building well-being.

Research on optimism and health

There is a significant body of research that links optimism to health. In a summary of the findings from 83 studies, optimism had a small to medium protection from death, poor cardiovascular out-comes, cancer, physical symptoms, or pain. This led the authors to see optimism as a significant predictor of positive health. Up to 10% of the variation in the likelihood of developing some health condition was due to optimism.

A recent study looking at over 97,000 postmenopausal women in the USA found that the most optimistic were less likely to develop coronary heart disease which included heart attacks, and angina. Also, fewer died, with 17 fewer deaths per 10,000 people during an eight-year period. Large studies such as this are very powerful, and provide good evidence that this is a real thing. And there seems no reason to not believe that these results are similar for men or younger women.

Evaluate your life using the PERMA model at regular intervals

Well-being and happiness are conditions most people are striving to achieve. Happiness is really only one part of well-being, and the PERMA acronym breaks down the processes into five elements to focus on to help you achieve and maximize your health and well-being. It is useful to think about this at regular intervals and look at where you could make improvements in your life. You probably understand the positive emotions, such as pleasure and content-

"Post-it" note technique

The PERMA model is a really useful way to look at your own life and so let's use this as a basis for this "post-it" note technique. Take five "post-it" notes and allocate one to each of the letters P . . . E . . . R . . . M . . . A. Take the first "post-it" note and write down three things that you do that give you positive emotions, for example spending time with friends or walking in the sunshine. Then write down three things you would like to start or do more of to increase your positive emotions. The next day take the second "post-it" note and do the same for the letter E, for engagement. Continue until you have completed all five letters. Don't worry if you can't think of three things for each letter; that is not important and some letters will probably feel more difficult than others.

Take a look at all five "post-it" notes and recognize how many things you already do that improve your well-being. You may want to add some of the new ideas you have identified to the list you made in the very first "post-it" note. Just trying one of these things can improve your well-being so give it a go!

ment, that will enhance your well-being. Engagement is more likely to be overlooked, but working on focus can lead to the experience of "flow". You'll notice the importance of positive and good relationships stressed throughout as these help to support you in your life. The "M" stands for meaning, as your endeavours will enhance your well-being further when there is some sort of meaning attached to them. Do you need to do more things to give you meaning in your life? And finally, achievements, when they match your expectations, will provide a positive feeling. These elements combined with optimism, as previously detailed within Chapter 2 "Challenge your thinking", will help generate positive feedback which will lead you to further achievements.

Chapter 8

SELF-ESTEEM

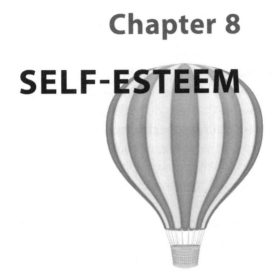

A local general practitioner, who had worked successfully for many years, was describing the difficulties he was having at work. "I feel like a fraud. I think to myself why are these people coming and asking for my help?" All the evidence pointed to him being highly qualified but he was unable to make this assessment of himself.

If I ask you "what does self-esteem mean?" what would you say? You could probably identify people you know who have high self-esteem, or conversely those with low self-esteem, but what is it about those people that led you to those conclusions? You develop your self-esteem during your childhood, but this does not make it fixed for the rest of your life. In this chapter we will be defining self-esteem and looking at what factors contribute to a healthy self-esteem. You can take responsibility for change.

Self-esteem is the opinion you have of yourself, your evaluation of your own worth. It is a combination of self-confidence and self-respect. It is your perception of your ability to deal with challenges in your life, to recognize and solve any problems, to believe you have a right to be happy and to feel worthy of respect. Do you apply any of the statements in the following box to yourself? Can you identify which statements are applicable to people with high self-esteem?

As mentioned, from childhood your self-esteem is a constantly evolving process of believing in yourself and understanding your self-worth. It is an ability to see your place in the world realistically and optimistically. You should aim to have the confidence to make changes and work towards getting better at whatever you choose to do.

The purpose of a strong and enduring self-esteem is that it transcends the short term, and the often unhelpful focus you can place on yourself in the world. The person with solid self-esteem loves

When you think about yourself, are you . . .

- Critical?
- Proud of your achievements?
- Downplaying or ignoring your positive qualities?
- Happy to tell others about how well you did?
- Judging yourself as inferior to your peers?
- Able to defend your views with others?
- Using negative words to describe yourself, such as stupid or fat?
- Assuming luck plays a large role in all of your achievements?
- Someone who blames yourself when things go wrong?
- Able to identify where things went wrong objectively?
- A person who believes compliments given to you?

by choice and there is not a sense of being in a relationship just because they have to, but from a secure base where both their needs and those of the other person are met.

Self-awareness is a useful skill

Self-awareness is defined as having an awareness of your thoughts and feelings in addition to your environment and others within it. As we have seen in Chapter 3 "Anger", being aware of your own emotional changes can help prevent behaving in a way that harms others. In Chapter 5 "Distress" we discussed how being aware of the normal physiological changes in your body can help prevent a spiralling panic. In both these instances you take responsibility for the reality of your body. Self-awareness is important in developing your self-esteem too, as it requires knowledge of the self, and acceptance of the areas that need improvement.

You might have difficulty becoming self-aware due to the current stressors in your environment, the intensity of your emotional responses, your personality, or even medical conditions. You can improve your self-awareness by looking at different areas of your life.

For example, you could choose to look at your physical appearance, both literally and figuratively, or your health. You could examine your achievements in life and the relationships you have made with other people. You could look more deeply at your connection with what is going on, with people and events, or you could examine your spirituality, not necessarily in a formal religious way but in how your beliefs interact with the world. This list is not exhaustive and you may recognize other areas you want to explore in order to develop your self-awareness. Within the examination of these things, you could note how they change over time, and allow yourself to develop goals in each of these areas of self-awareness. This also encourages a love of learning about yourself and the world.

Self-esteem can be improved both from external and internal influences

External factors that encourage the development of self-esteem can come in the form of praise from others, awards for recognized successes, and possessions that demonstrate social status. The problem with solely building your self-esteem on external factors is that praise from others is subject to something outside your control. If you only based your self-esteem on external factors then you would only see yourself as successful if others thought that you were. But there are several ways that you can improve your own internally generated self-esteem. Nathaniel Branden, a leader in the field of self-esteem research, has identified a framework for how self-esteem is constructed internally in his book *The Six Pillars of Self-esteem* (2004). These are: living consciously, self-acceptance, self-responsibility, self-assertiveness, living purposefully, personal integrity. Let's take a closer look at these as a structure you can use to improve your self-esteem.

The first pillar is conscious living, identified by most spiritual traditions as the objective of life and the way to live life. Conscious living, also referred to as mindfulness, is being aware of things. Some people think that mindfulness should leave the person trying to have an "empty" mind. This is far from the truth, and the practice is about being aware, aware of how your body feels, your emotional feelings, what sounds and sights are around you, and all of this whilst it is happening. This will be discussed further in Chapter 10 "Relaxation techniques".

Developing self-acceptance, both good and bad, will improve self-esteem

A second part of self-esteem is captured with the term self-acceptance. This is believing in oneself, and perceiving the positive aspects of your personality accurately and favourably. It also involves accurately acknowledging your weaknesses, and accepting these with the knowledge that you are able to improve these aspects of yourself. How much do you believe in the following statement?

> I acknowledge my faults. I like myself. Some of the things I do are unhelpful. An example of this is . . . and some of the things I do are very helpful to both me and to others.

The way you reflect on this statement will help you to orientate yourself in relation to your feelings of self-acceptance. Being able to rate aspects of your personality that you are looking to improve provides the first step.

You could imagine that social exclusion would impact negatively on a person's self-esteem; however, a meta-analysis by Blackhart and colleagues in 2009 identified some surprising findings. Looking at studies of interpersonal rejection and ostracism, the rejection felt caused people to shift their mood. This makes sense despite the fact that the result, generally, is an emotionally neutral state. This is seen in outcomes of low levels of both positive and negative mood. Now the importance here is self-acceptance which causes an increase in positive mood and improves self-esteem. The rejection itself doesn't lead to differences in self-esteem, however, responding realistically to the rejection, measured in your acceptance of it, is the key.

Self-confidence is a belief in oneself as a person, leading to a general sense of "I can do it" or what others have described as "having grit". Grit, also known as resilience, refers to the perseverance required to meet long-term goals and is often immune to the little setbacks that accompany any journey. This is important when thinking about competence, as demonstrating competence is all well and good, but it is not a way to establish self-esteem by itself. If you solely base feelings of self-esteem on your competence and achievements, then when you fail there are no internal structures present with which to build self-esteem.

Michael Crowley developed an interesting model looking at the interactions between our own self-evaluation and the vulnerability we have to evaluations made by other people. He observed that those people with high vulnerability to the evaluations of others, irrespective of their own self-evaluations, were often "people pleasers", had difficulty saying no, and avoided stressful interactions with others at all costs. Those with the dual burden of a low self-evaluation and a high vulnerability to the evaluations of other people felt helplessness in meeting their own needs and indeed the perceived needs of others.

The outcomes are up to you

Self-responsibility means taking responsibility that the outcomes of your achievements are due to you, and not the product of chance, hope, or luck. When thinking about responsibility you must also think about self-control. In one paper by VanDellen et al. in 2012, it was found that self-esteem moderated the relationship between social rejection and lowered self-control. When you face rejection in a social situation, your mood suffers and your view of your own level of control in a situation can suffer too. Interestingly this is often only among individuals with low self-esteem and in specific circumstances. When something has no social implications, people with low self-esteem don't care as much. Research suggests individuals with low self-esteem exert more effort on tasks of social value. What we can take from this is that having a clear measure of how much you are bothered by other people's evaluations of you is important for your mood. It is especially important if you have low self-esteem.

Self-assertiveness is implicit to your human rights

The Universal Declaration of Human Rights, in 1948, was the first of its kind identifying the rights all humans were entitled to. Coming out of the atrocities leading up to and including the Second World War, this applied to all people without exception. The emphasis here is important, and taking a look at the first article it states "All human beings are born free and equal in dignity and rights. They are endowed with reason and conscience and should act towards one another in a spirit of brotherhood." Now this seems like something everyone can agree on. However, when you fail to express your thoughts, feelings, and beliefs, and permit others to violate your rights, you set aside this important declaration.

It might also be less obvious to identify, but when you express your views in an apologetic, self-effacing manner, it prompts others to easily disregard your rights. It is your responsibility to be assertive, standing up for yourself and being able to express how you feel. Passivity, which leads to a lack of respect for your needs, is like saying "my feelings don't matter". You are appeasing others just to avoid conflict. Not only do you not get your needs met, but also others will lose respect for you.

Having purpose in your efforts improves self-esteem

Living purposely, the fifth of the six pillars, relates to planning ways to achieve your goals. This involves, first, defining those goals and then, formulating and carrying out actions to complete them. The importance of having a purpose has been demonstrated in research on people with spinal cord injury. Graham will explain the research in the following box.

On a lighter note, Freud once said that love and work are the cornerstones of our "humanness". I notice people often make a mess of their love lives yet shine at work. Let's use this as a task to help focus on love and establish its purpose, the same kind of purpose people often find in work. Imagine for a moment if you were to approach both work and love with the same vigour. It would be interesting to see what the impact would be.

Purposeful life impacts in life for people with injury

There are serious adjustments required by those with spinal cord injury, where trauma rather than disease can cause loss of physical functions in a person. The recovery from these sorts of injury involves the very psychological resources we are discussing here. A systematic literature review of 83 studies showed that self-esteem was consistently associated with positive adjustment indicators such as high well-being and improved mental health. Having a purpose in life was found to positively determine the adjustment outcomes measured in this group that had faced significant life stressors.

Imagine you are applying for the job of being your partner's love interest. What type of job would it be? Would it be administrative, have a marketing component, involve the construction of love, or its engineering? Would you see yourself as a doctor might in healthcare, looking after love, prolonging love and treating its symptoms when it becomes ill? Or as a technician might in Information Services, or as a scientist might, experimenting with love.

What are the knowledge, skills, and abilities needed to be in a loving relationship? What kind of general knowledge of love do you have? What experiences in love have you had and can bring to the current position? How many years of experience have you had and do you have any specialized training in love? What kind of love training do you plan to have?

With our paid work we often have primary objectives which help identify our goals. For love – where do you want to be in love in five years? Break down these goals into the details like your values, how you express your love, or the number of times you say "I love you". How do you measure performance and improve love? How do you comply with others' views of love?

Often when writing a resume we describe our interests. How do the things you do or the people you associate with improve your love with your partner? How do they get in the way? What are the physical demands of love? For example, while performing the responsibilities of the job of love, the employee is required to communicate effectively and listen. Could you handle this work? In answering the questions above it exposes and clarifies your purpose in love and gets down to the nuts and bolts of what it takes to keep yourself employed in the job of love.

Personal integrity is consistency with your values

Integrity is derived from the Latin adjective "integer" that we still use in English. This means complete, whole, fully formed, and reflects how a person is when they have integrity. More specifically, it is a situation where you adhere to your own internal ethics and morals. This is the opposite of hypocrisy, and we value this virtue in people.

A useful exercise is to identify your goals in terms of your values. These might be things like honesty, respecting family, or indeed humour. In identifying values, we can get a clearer idea as to the thought barriers that exist. For example, if you value honesty then how does that fit into your statements about yourself? Can you honestly say you are the most important person in your life because without you, it is not possible to fulfil the roles you have chosen of mother, brother, or indeed friend? Similarly, if you respect your family and the views they have, how is it that you can reject or minimize their compliments when they come your way? Count the number of times you hear "yeah . . . but" in answering these questions.

Deci and Ryan (1995) note that intrinsic aspirations are associated with positive mental health. They note personal growth, meaningful relationships, and community contributions not only match the definition of a person who is secure in themselves, but these areas are also good unto themselves. As we have noted before, the way one increases the likelihood of feeling good is to do something for someone else.

Realistic thinking helps your self-esteem

As we saw in Chapter 6 "Unhappiness", errors in thinking are associated with lower mood. One example is emotional reasoning, or your reliance on the way you feel to determine the way you act. This reliance also affects the way you think about yourself. This has obvious implications for self-esteem. An example might be the understanding that if you feel stupid, therefore you are stupid or if you feel inferior to other people, then other people are better than you are. When I first started therapy, I often had the following anxious thought. I imagined that as a young therapist I would be half way through a session and the "Psychology Police", an imaginary organization of crack psychologists who enforced the "Psychology Laws", would burst open the door and say "Stop what you are doing, there has been a terrible mistake, you should never have been allowed to provide therapy. You are doing it all wrong and we are going to take away all your degrees and the sign on your door saying Psychologist." Funnily enough, this hasn't happened in all my years as a therapist. You will also have times when you feel less confident about your abilities and question your worth.

Just as my bank balance can fluctuate, everyone lacks the confidence they need sometimes. However, some people with chronic low self-esteem are unhappy or unsatisfied with themselves most of the time, irrespective of their achievements or the opinions of others. As we have seen in Chapters 5 "Distress" and 6 "Unhappiness", not taking responsibility for the positive outcomes of life, as well as the negative outcomes, negatively influences your mood. There is some strong evidence that low self-esteem can cause mood problems, including depression and anxiety.

Everyone has times when they feel that they cannot cope. The skills and attributes required are badged under the phrase "emotional resilience". This is where you can cope with stress as it comes your way, and have the ability to bounce back. This resilience is needed by me within my job, and I am sure you will have times when you need to do the same.

As part of this, humour is a very important device in life. When you say negative things about yourself and hold very serious views about how good you are – where is the humour? It is very important to identify and challenge beliefs which damage self-esteem. This is interesting as you will be making the definite distinction between your thoughts and who you really are. If the thoughts you are having are getting in the way of healthy self-esteem then it is your responsibility to change these thoughts. Some of these thoughts include not being able to commit to social outings, where you can't make decisions regarding a time to meet or you can't make decisions because of how you might feel if you do go. How does your choice about procrastination get in the way of healthy self-esteem?

Healthy boundaries protect self-esteem

The boundaries related to your self-esteem are what you take ownership for and what belongs to other people. A useful analogy here is to think of the property boundary of your house. The items inside the boundary are the things you have worked hard for and what makes your house unique. From this analogy, these items within your house are personal just like the feelings and emotions that reside inside of you. This notion can be helpful in also working out what belongs to other people. Just as you are not likely to reach over and borrow your neighbour's toothbrush, there are some things that are best left on the other side of the fence. You can clearly recognize when a boundary has been crossed and also when you have been invited to do so. Just like a written invitation to a housewarming party at your neighbour's house, crossing the personal boundary of another person is clear – you know the time, place, and dress code.

In relationships, where there are unclear boundaries, there are various processes which make it difficult to establish where one person ends and another person begins. Like all things that are dynamic and living, good boundaries are able to breathe. In healthy families, the difference between a parent and a child is clear, which allows the parent and child to play together, negotiate, and lay down rules when required. Children benefit from being independent and autonomous in this way and are then able to more fully socialize when with their friends, while having their basic needs for love and nurturing met at home. To paraphrase Tolstoy, happy families are all alike; every unhappy family is unhappy in its own way. Unhappy families exhibit chaos, where it is hard to tell the parent from the child, the child from the parent.

Boundaries relate to self-esteem as they serve a purpose. When the rights of all are respected, the person is able to express themselves without fear of being neglected or abused. Part of self-esteem management is identifying the things you are doing which get in the way of healthy self-esteem. Often there are many reasons why you don't express your needs, feelings, and desires. You may think that not expressing your opinion isn't that much of a problem and won't get you into trouble. By not initiating a conversation, then you can avoid that uncomfortable feeling when the awkward silence descends halfway through.

This type of thinking can lead you to think that you have no control over any or indeed all aspects of your life. It can lead you to not attempting new adventures and experiences. But what you are doing by these actions is violating those terms of the Universal Declaration of Human Rights. Yes, this seems extreme but the Charter is very clear. As Article One stated, when you say you don't have a right to express your feelings or that another person's rights are more important than yours, you are in direct violation of these rights.

Measuring improvements will allow you to keep track of progress

Measuring self-esteem in practice is often hard; it is difficult to pin down change. Often, people notice just feeling better about themselves without seeing where this has changed their behaviour. A patient once said it wasn't their motivation that was a problem getting to the gym, but rather their willpower. Now I hear you asking "what is the difference?" That is a good question, as often they are used interchangeably. Willpower is your own determination to achieve something, to complete a difficult task, or an easy task. It is generated within yourself. Motivation comes from your response to outside stimuli – these can be positive or negative forces, but they then result in action. For example, if you decide to give up smoking, your motivation comes from the health implications, other people around you and their feelings, and the financial costs. But, the willpower you will require must come from yourself, and will be tested in the course of trying to quit.

To further explore this, we find that by increasing your awareness of these positive attributes like motivation and indeed willpower, you are able to work out and manage them in the same way you manage other areas of your life. Your understanding of this attribute is another strength. Insight into how your behaviour changes when your self-esteem is low can help you avoid placing yourself in risky situations. Conversely, when your self-esteem is high you are able to take advantage of this knowledge and take on challenges which take you outside of your comfort zone.

"Post-it" note technique

Think about positive aspects of yourself and your life. Take a "post-it" note and write down three positive things about yourself. These can be attributes, things about you. They could be achievements, things you have completed, or anything else that is positive. Try to make sure they are about *you*. Don't fall into the trap of giving yourself credit for something that relates to someone or something else. Credit for your child's or pet's personality is not something you should class as self-esteem. Try repeating this process each day. You may find this difficult to do at first and it may feel very unnatural. However with practice it becomes easier and spending time recognizing these positive things about yourself will have a beneficial effect on your self-esteem.

Confidence and worth are the basic tenets of self-esteem. It is your responsibility to measure your self-esteem and change it if necessary. By doing this, you build the very foundations that can help you weather the storms which come from facing the things you have previously avoided. Living each day in the moment, living with purpose, accepting your strengths and your limitations all help in establishing the boundaries that are both your right and your responsibility to maintain.

Chapter 9

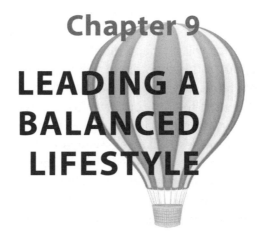

LEADING A
BALANCED
LIFESTYLE

"Everything in moderation, including moderation."
(Oscar Wilde, possibly)

Providing space for, and being content with, your life is at the heart of having a balanced lifestyle. Feeling good is more easily achieved when all of the elements in your life are in balance. The balance you strive for will be dependent upon your circumstances and lifestyle, but in this chapter we will try to provide some pointers. In simple terms, when there are two things to balance it is fairly straightforward to work out how to achieve a balance. As with the see-saw introduced in Chapter 5 "Distress", equal pressure on either side provides a balance. Saying that, even with good balance, there will always be a sway with small movements but these don't represent poor balance and are easily corrected. If only your world were this simple. There are many more than two things to balance at any one time in your life, and this is where the challenge arises.

Moderation is one way of approaching a balanced lifestyle. As with the see-saw effect, pressing down too much on one side which can be considered to be a lack of moderation, leads to an imbalance. This issue of being moderate in life has been replicated by many people and within many cultures. The argument against this approach seems to revolve around the difficulty in defining moderation for an individual. For example, one person's moderate level of eating may be another person's excess. But this is not to say that there is a global standard for moderation in every aspect in life. In truth, you probably know what is moderation for yourself. In striving to achieve this, balance is more likely.

The phrase "work-life balance" hides a range of issues

Let's start with a much discussed phrase, in the media, politics, and workplaces around the world. A "work-life balance" sounds fair and intuitive, in that your work and the rest of your life should be balanced. This is not a new concept, as it was proposed in the 1800s that a "work-leisure" balance was something to strive for, with the more modern phrase used since the 1980s.

Balance, as mentioned earlier, would be easier if work and life were truly constructed from two things in opposition. But of course your work impacts on your time, energy levels, money, relationships, worthwhile achievements, and ambition to state just a few. This conflicts with the time and energy you have reserved for your lifestyle, which encompasses your family and friends, children, socializing, reading, doing good things, exercise, entertainment, even further education. There are also clearly places for overlap between your work and your life, for example in socializing. Over the past ten years there has been further blurring of the distinction between work and home life, particularly with technical advances. Let's look at one example. As I write these words, I am sat in my house working on a laptop connected to the internet. I am receiving a continual stream of emails which are diverting my attention. I have mixed a home space with a working environment. I am not unique. Many of you will have done just this.

These things are a challenge. How do you balance them? One approach, taken by many people and more often by women, is to reduce the number of hours of paid work. This may improve the situation but only in conjunction with other techniques. Depending on your context, you can develop ways to control work dominating home and personal life, which I group into three areas: challenge your thinking, maintain your boundaries, and access support.

Challenging your thinking

The importance of achievement, and the thoughts in relation to achievement, in influencing our self-efficacy were described in

Chapter 4 "Self-efficacy". Often people will try to achieve many things in their life but judge themselves by one criterion. You may feel that, if a task was not completed in the time allocated, it means the task wasn't done. Again, if it is not as perfect as you would like it to be, does that mean the flaws or mistakes make it unusable? Did you learn anything from the journey as well? This desire for perfection in one part of your life must be balanced, in a working sense, with other parts of your life. Striving to achieve, no matter what, is by its definition an impossible way to develop a balanced lifestyle. Paid work time is very different from time at home in your personal life, but you should be careful not to use excessive work as a form of escape from things happening in other parts of your life.

Maintaining your boundaries

There is growing evidence that the balance is shifting towards more work, and consequently an imbalance with the rest of your life. A report published by Natalie Skinner and colleagues in 2012 found that women's lives seem to be more affected, particularly with western society's expectation that women work along with men. Some techniques that can prove useful are to leave work at the workplace, at least sometimes. Try to not clutter your home environment with work stuff. Some people try very hard to make sure they return from work at an appropriate time, leaving time for your friends and family to see you. The emails flying around the ether are a great distraction, and the advent of smartphones that have you connected 24 hours a day don't let you easily escape. Experiment with strategies such as leaving your phone at home when you go to socialize, or turning the phone to silent. Be mindful of the times you often unconsciously reach to browse your emails.

Accessing support

Many of these techniques will also require you to be assertive with yourself, and possibly with others. You will be surprised how often other people accept your demands for a better balance in your work-life environment. This is when you should access support from wherever it is available. Often these forms of support, in both your work and home life, are informal, based on kindness and humanity. Employers have a level of duty of care that has various degrees of formality depending on where you are working. Employee assistance programmes are being developed around the world, which encourage employers to help their workers to stay as healthy as possible. These programmes will provide and have provided a good return on investment for businesses, improving the productivity of their employees, so everyone gains.

Controlling things you can change

Issues of control, or lack of it, are common triggers for mood issues. The need to feel less vulnerable is a strong driver for the need for control. The Serenity Prayer, of which an extract is given in the box on the following page, was written by Reinhold Niebuhr and describes some of the feelings associated with control, and some of those emotions you may feel when you realize you do not have control. Niebuhr had a difficult journey himself, but influenced Dr Martin Luther King and his words are also echoed in Alcoholics Anonymous meetings around the globe.

The poem describes how there are some things you can change and some things you cannot. This seems obvious. However it is worth further exploration. Firstly, by identifying where each of the work/life issues you are dealing with lies in terms of ability to change, this will then allow you to accept those beyond your

Serenity Prayer (extract)

God grant me the serenity
to accept the things I cannot change;
courage to change the things I can;
and wisdom to know the difference.
Living one day at a time;
enjoying one moment at a time;
accepting hardships as the pathway to peace . . .
by Reinhold Niebuhr

control. The poem continues with a call of strength and courage to deal with things that you can control. Assertiveness and using your strengths to attain balance are key elements. The next part of the poem speaks of a mindful approach to life, one day at a time, one moment at a time. No need to be concerned with things too far ahead, enjoy the here and now. This is a way of living that ties in with many other cultures. Examples expressing similar sentiments to the Serenity Prayer can be found in Buddhism, Islam, or Christianity. The next box is an example written by an 8th-century Indian Buddhist scholar called Shantideva of Nalanda University.

"If there's a remedy when trouble strikes . . ."

If there's a remedy when trouble strikes,
What reason is there for dejection?
And if there is no help for it,
What use is there in being glum?
by Shantideva of Nalanda University

Develop your motivation for change

Achieving balance in your life requires you to change your behaviours. The difficulties that this poses, and the uncertainty of the value of the outcome, may lead you to ambivalence: you may be undecided whether you wish to change a behaviour. This is where motivation is key. Motivational Interviewing (MI) is a therapy with motivation at its core.

Formal MI requires two people, you and a therapist. I hear you ask "how will this help me?" The principles that MI uses will be helpful for you working by yourself, to develop motivation, and be aware of, and then move away from, ambivalence. Many of the core aspects of MI are driven by the person and not the therapist, and so this is within your grasp. An understanding of MI will help you to get ready to challenge your behaviour, and allow you to be specific when asking the vital next question "what am I going to do about it?"

MI is about the stages of change a person goes through on their journey whilst they are challenging a behaviour. When you try to change a behaviour you move through stages described as pre-contemplation, contemplation, determination and action, maintenance, and relapse. Which stage the person has reached and what they are thinking about change are, for the therapist, very important variables in the equation in helping them to get to where they want to be.

To move from one stage to the next you must decide that you do not want to continue to be where you are. Building motivation to move from a stage might require a difficult question: does your life have the endurance to continue with these painful and difficult emotions? If you stay where you are now, which often feels the easiest option, then you are saying that you can handle more of what is going on right now, more distress, and more frustration. Often you spend all your time trying to avoid unpleasant emotions having a short-term focus without thinking about the implications for the longer term. Acceptance, which is a key aspect to mindfulness and a range of other therapies, teaches you to allow these unpleasant sensations to come and go without struggle and allows you to understand yourself better.

Let's look at the example of stopping smoking. This is a classic issue for people's mood, and presents a whole range of difficulties. The goal is the permanent cessation of the problem behaviour; the usefulness of MI is that it matches the majority of people's experiences, where relapse is likely and people often get back on the horse they just fell off.

When setting goals it is important to know what works. Kivetz and colleagues in 2006 built on the work of the behaviourist Hull and found that the effort invested in achieving a goal is a function of the proportion of the original distance remaining to the goal. We know that laboratory rats, and indeed people, get faster in what they are doing the closer they get to a goal. The perception of distance to the goal is important as even when the number of behaviours is the same, any perceived progress toward the goal impacts on your behaviour.

To illustrate this, imagine there are two coffee shops, one where you must buy eight coffees to get a free coffee and the other where you must buy ten. With all eight coffees to buy before your next free coffee from the first coffee shop, you are less motivated and buy fewer coffees than if you need ten coffees and you have already bought two, with eight remaining. The distance is the same, eight coffees, but the proportion is different, with one needing all 100% and the other only 80%. Less psychological distance is created which means our behaviour changes which in turn means behaviour is different.

There are four principles to MI. The first is to express empathy, which for a therapist is an important role. But how do you do that on your own? This is known as self-empathy, and involves you listening to your own situation, and accepting it for what it is. Returning to the example of giving up smoking, accept that you are currently a smoker and be realistic about how much you smoke, how much of your time and money are spent on this behaviour. Ask yourself, am I the only person who has ever had to face this challenge?

The second principle is to identify a gap between where you are and where you want to be, which you can do for yourself. This needs to come from you but as we have seen this can be difficult for people to do by themselves. MI looks to help you question how your current behaviour compares with the behaviours of the person you want to be. How will it feel to be a non-smoker?

The third principle is that MI looks to get you to roll with the punches in changing a behaviour or in more psychological terms, deal with "resistance". This is a natural way you use to justify the very behaviour you are looking to stop and often involves several arguments. Smoking helps me deal with stress. I've tried stopping before and it hasn't worked. Even when I stopped for a few months I went back to it again. You may not understand if you don't smoke. Here the key is not challenging the reasoning used, as we know from previous chapters it is full of bias and likely to be flawed. The key to MI is avoiding arguments; research using MI, published by Miller in 1993, has found that an increase in the arguments between therapist and client or indeed the use of confrontation increases the resistance shown or worse still increases the problem behaviour the person first came to see the therapist about. Maybe you could explore different ways to deal with stress other than smoking. Hopefully you have learnt a few strategies as you've worked through this book. This is a less confrontational approach than challenging the reasoning that smoking helps deal with stress.

Build an accurate view of you

The final principle in MI is about building self-esteem to improve the confidence required to get things done. Ways to improve self-esteem have been looked at in Chapter 8 "Self-esteem". In previous chapters you have learnt that old habits form blinkers to new experience. People may have varied motivations to change. Some are external to us and range from a friend making a simple suggestion or a threat from a partner that if "you don't get help, I am leaving you". On the inside a recognition that there are things in your life you would like to change can be recognized as a strength and acted upon with confidence. The outcome is the same: people act on their motivation and seek help to improve.

Pleasant event scheduling is designed to improve mood

"Pleasant event scheduling" is often used successfully in therapy to change routines and challenge existing habits. The process involves listing activities that give you pleasure, for example, going to the cinema, taking a long bath, eating your favourite meal, and from this list selecting a small number to schedule into your weekly routine. The aim is to improve your general mood and also challenge the expectations you have about your mood and what is possible in your week. This has a myriad of benefits from giving you something to look forward to, breaking the cycle of inactivity and casting doubt on negative beliefs about yourself, and eroding your self-criticisms. It is a useful technique to develop insight, getting you to exist a little outside of yourself.

The importance of sleep is underestimated

Sleep is difficult for a large number of people. Recent surveys suggest that up to one third of us suffer from insomnia, with even more of us having occasional poor sleep. Sleep is elusive and seems to slip further from the person's grasp the more they try and grab it. Graham, in the next box, explains the importance of sleep and its impact on health. It is curious how science has mostly ignored the role of sleep in the development and maintenance of health, although this is now beginning to change.

When you have poor sleep, one of the ways to deal with this is to use advice on "sleep hygiene". Advice from the UK's National Health Service on this suggests a number of things:

- Establish a fixed time for going to bed and waking up, but have some flexibility to make sure you only really go to bed when you feel sleepy.
- Avoid the temptation to sleep longer the night after a poor night's sleep.
- Try to relax before going to bed.
- Ensure that your bedroom is comfortable, uncluttered, cool, and quiet.
- Avoid taking a nap during the day.
- Do not drink caffeine after 12 noon.
- Avoid nicotine and alcohol at night.
- Consider exercising in the middle of the day, but avoid exercise in the evening.

We know you need sleep

The only thing we know about sleep with certainty is that humans need to sleep. A dreadful genetic disorder, known as Fatal Familial Insomnia, suffered by only a handful of people, robs the sufferer of the ability to sleep. Within six months, and often a far shorter time, those suffering from this disease have died. Their dying days are spent in pain that medical science has been unable to deal with. This is the extreme, but it does make us think that we should see sleep as an essential nutrient, in much the same way as breathing, water, and food are essential.

People with insomnia, or a difficulty in initiating or maintaining sleep, report lower quality of life than people without insomnia. They do worse on cognitive measures and also on their health-related quality of life. They suffer significantly more symptoms of depression and anxiety and their work and other activities of daily living are affected. Obesity and poor cardiovascular health has been linked with poor quality sleep. Unfortunately at the moment science has been unable to determine whether poor sleep actually causes poor health, but the biology and physiology predicts that it does.

When asleep we know that there is REM (Rapid Eye Movement) sleep where the majority of dreaming occurs and then non-REM sleep where there are different levels of sleep, the deepest being stage 4 from which it is the most difficult to wake people. Problems in the balance of the chemical messenger systems responsible for sleep are disrupted by physiological, biological, and behavioural factors.

- Try to maintain a routine including eating, and avoid a heavy meal late at night.
- Use the bedroom mainly for sleep and sex.

In terms of your pattern of sleep, if you are unable to fall asleep within 15 minutes, get out of bed and try again later. Use deep breathing and muscle relaxation exercises to divert the mind from anxious thoughts and list making, which interfere with falling asleep. If you feel angry and frustrated because you can't sleep, don't try harder and harder to fall asleep. Turn on the light and do something different (but no electronics or rigorous exercise!).

Strategies for developing better sleep to help well-being

There are a number of ways you can work on the quantity and quality of your sleep. Sleep has many facets that scientists believe are important. A simple measure of sleep is the length of time you spend asleep. We can all pick a number of hours that we feel is our "standard", with on average people reporting approximately 8 hours of sleep. This amount varies considerably between people, with reports of between 6 and 10 hours per night. There are many people who routinely sleep even less than this. Throughout adult life, the amount of sleep we need gradually reduces as we grow older. This shows that there is no "standard" and that everyone has their own patterns of sleep quantity. Medical conditions, psychological problems such as depression and anxiety, and shift work can also drastically affect sleep, as does pain. There are also many things that you cannot change that affect your sleep. It has been often recognized that women report worse sleep than men.

Along with sleep quantity, the quality of your sleep is important. If you wake frequently during the night, or suffer from a condition such as Restless Legs Syndrome (RLS), this can reduce how energetic you feel the following day. The quality of your sleep can be measured with simple questionnaires, or using complex and expensive laboratory equipment. Measures of sleep quality include whether you are able to fall asleep within 30 minutes of getting into bed and trying to sleep. This can be one of the most troubling parts of a person's sleep habits. Other measures include frequent waking during the night, and feeling sleepy and unmotivated during the day.

Regular schedules have a role to play in improving mood

Daily exercise which is gentle but regular develops the rhythms needed for good quality sleep. As we mentioned above, the time a person goes to sleep matters. Shift workers are prone to excessively long times in bed but often experience fragmented and shallow sleep. By having a regular sleep time and wake-up time in the morning, we strengthen the association between the bed and sleep. We also strengthen the circadian cycling that leads to regular times of sleep onset, so that the physiological and biological processes can work effectively.

This is where, ironically, an alarm clock can help to develop a schedule, which your body will react to with hormonal and psychological changes that improve health. Regular mealtimes seem to be important too, including eating breakfast. A significant minority of people skip breakfast each day but imagine this – if I were to say to you that you are not allowed to eat for the next 17 hours what would you say? Is it possible? Would you be able to do it? This is exactly what people are doing when they skip "breaking the fast" associated with sleep. If you have dinner then don't eat until lunch the next day, this equals approximately 17 hours of time with no nutrition. When you do finally sit down to lunch after missing breakfast you make poorer food choices and your body suffers. A set time getting up each day and having breakfast sets the body to realizing that the nocturnal period has stopped and daytime has begun.

Yoga is a metaphor for balance

The practice of yoga is an ancient set of exercises, for both body and mind, that have become increasingly practised in western societies. The word yoga can be literally translated as union, where opposing forces present in your life are blended. There is a posture, known as tree, which is a simple pose but requires balance. The yoga practitioner stands on both feet and places the hands together, in a prayer position. Then he stands on one foot, and places the other foot on the inside of the thigh of the standing leg.

This posture requires some strength, a focus for the mind and the eyes, an understanding of your body and how it is aligned. Quite often very small adjustments are needed to remain in balance. More advanced practitioners then close their eyes, and remain balanced. This requires you to release control from your vision, and use other parts of your body to maintain the posture.

There have now been many studies of the pivotal role that yoga and other traditions can play in improving health. Graham describes some of these findings in the following box. These include the practice of the physical aspects of yoga, the breathing exercises, and other practices such as tai chi.

The scientific evidence for yoga and health

There is increasing evidence for the benefits of yoga, tai chi, and breathing exercises. Moliver found in 2013 that in a study of female yoga practitioners aged between 45 and 80, psychological well-being was improved. There was also a dose-response effect, which means the more you are exposed to something, the bigger the effect. In other words, the more yoga the better the well-being measures were that were reported. This was, however, an observational study which has some scientific drawbacks.

To overcome these shortfalls, a randomized controlled trial was conducted by Field in 2012 where 92 pregnant women who had suffered previously from depression were randomly assigned to tai chi/yoga or to nothing. The tai chi/yoga group did a 20-minute class weekly for 12 weeks. When the treatments were over, the tai chi/yoga group had lower depression scores, lower negative mood scores and fewer somatic/vegetative symptoms, reduced anxiety, and less sleep disturbance.

There are many forms of yoga, but one that forms part of many types of yoga is what is sometimes referred to as "karma yoga". This can be translated into a yoga of selfless service, and relies on altruistic practices, but must not be based on any particular outcome for the practitioner. For example I have heard about people working in a yoga school for no payment, to help the school to operate and to enhance the enjoyment of those attending the school. Seeing this can have a profound psychological effect on those watching this kindness, making the world seem a better place. This is similar to the concept of "random acts of kindness" where a person does something for someone else for no reason other than to help out that other person.

These practices bring a higher level of contentment to the person practising the kindness. Indeed, in my experience, the acts themselves give more back to the person doing the kind acts, than to the person on the receiving end.

"Post-it" note technique

It's time to record a little bit of karma yoga that you have earned. Take a "post-it" note, and write down something that you have done today for someone else. Hopefully it will be something that you are not being paid for, something that you did as a random act of kindness. Do this for five days in a row. You can feel very proud of doing this. Notice the positive effects of reading these at the end of the week. Perhaps it will encourage you to do this more often?

How do I stay here?

So, you have now achieved the state of balance you have been striving for. How do you maintain this? Feeling good, in a deep and meaningful way, does not fall into your lap without you putting time and energy into this activity. You have arrived at this chapter and so have already put a great deal of effort into reading and hopefully working through the "post-it" note techniques. On top of arriving where you want to be, you need all the things in place to prevent a relapse. Your mood, and the inevitable changes in your mood, will be there for your entire life. As mentioned, your mood changes constantly but you should now have some strategies to deal with a difficult mood and prevent it spiralling out of control. Setbacks are normal. They provide an opportunity to practise skills you have acquired and are important in the resilience associated with a healthy balanced lifestyle.

"Post-it" note technique

One of the commonly mentioned problems is that your mind is too busy when you close your eyes at night and this prevents you drifting off to sleep. When your room is quiet, your mind is often a noisy place thinking of all the things that have happened that day or the things you need to do the following day or just a time to worry. This is a good opportunity to try out a useful writing technique. Before you go to bed, if there is something worrying you or a thought you can't get out of your mind, write it down. Use a "post-it" note and write down your worry or thought on it.

Pin the note up and leave it. Think of the problem as on-hold; it is not going anywhere, and it will still be there in the morning. There is nothing to be done with this problem now. Keep thinking this, and try to not let your mind wander when your head finally rests on the pillow. If the thought appears in your mind then try to label it "thought" and discard it.

This all leads back to what we said at the start about balance. Even when things are in perfect balance, there is an inevitable sway in the system. Things change, you move to a new job, have children who grow up and then leave home. This is analogous to the constant changes in your mood and when things challenge your balance you must deal with these changes as time passes. These changes are a natural consequence of life, and should not knock you away from your plan to achieve balance.

With this in mind, it's important to plan for setbacks on your journey. Even thinking about these setbacks can be useful to identify the types of self-doubts which trouble your thoughts. In this book, we hope that you have developed the skills required to cope with setbacks by yourself.

Chapter 10

RELAXATION TECHNIQUES

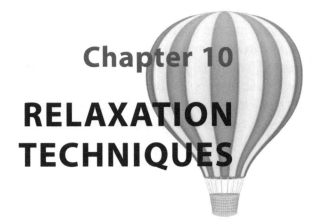

I was talking with a 55-year-old builder about his experience of using specific techniques for relaxation. I asked "Did you notice any changes in your body?" and he said "I was sinking further back into the chair and my toes got cold. My breathing was more relaxed, and I didn't need as much oxygen and I could feel my heart slowing down." I then asked "Where did your mind go?" and he replied "Really just on the breath and thinking of how far I used to get my heart rate down. When I really focussed, I could get it down to the 40s and maybe if I relax enough, I can get it back down there. I guess I felt a bit more in control."

Relaxation is control. It is showing yourself and indeed others that you have mastered your emotions. By controlling how you think and how you feel, relaxation helps you in many different ways. You feel better immediately when you relax properly. That one moment in your day when your breathing rate slows down, you drop your shoulders, and you sink further down into the chair. Relaxation also helps to prevent and control the feelings that frighten you. By successfully practising relaxation you can improve your belief in your ability to cope, therefore improving your self-efficacy, as discussed in Chapter 4 "Self-efficacy".

This chapter will discuss breathing exercises, progressive muscle relaxation, and mindfulness. By the end of this chapter you will have practised the skills required to relax, be able to recognize any signs and symptoms of stress, and start to implement relaxation into your life. How you apply the techniques to your life is up to you as an individual: everybody does it slightly differently. What is common to everyone is that the benefit achieved from using these techniques is related to the degree of effort you are prepared to put in.

Relaxation and mindfulness exercises allow you to be free to explore all parts of your world, both what is happening within you and outside in the broader physical world surrounding it. In this chapter you'll learn about several techniques and how practising these techniques can help in managing mood problems.

As discussed in Chapter 5 "Distress", one of the first symptoms in a panic episode is an increase in the breathing rate. This is an extreme example of how important your breathing is. The breathing exercises discussed here aim to control the physical aspects of distress. We will also look at the control of worry and negative thinking by using mindfulness.

Relaxation is freedom

When I talk about relaxation I am talking about freedom. This refers to freedom in your mind, an ability to work through issues to feel good. To illustrate this, an ancient Greek philosopher, Epictetus, said "No man is free who is not a master of himself". You can also take heart in what Aristotle is reported to have said in that "I count him braver who overcomes his desires than him who conquers his enemies; for the hardest victory is over self". So, freedom through conquering yourself is difficult but worth the effort.

Relaxation is the focusing of attention and the heightening of concentration. When you focus your attention you narrow the scope of your thinking to one area; for example "I am thinking about relaxing the muscles in my legs". When you narrow the scope you are less likely to think about the milk and bread you need to get on the way home from the office. These other thoughts will often come up and that is OK. In the following box I compare your mind to a child, and draw parallels with concentration and relaxation difficulties you may have.

Your mind as a baby

When was the last time you walked with a child? As you remember, when you walk with a child they are keen to explore, are curious, and lead you on a merry chase everywhere except where you want to go. In order to get the child to go where you want to go there are two options. You could physically force the child to head in the direction you want by punishment. Now obviously this is rarely, if ever, acceptable, and may be child abuse, which leads to massive problems for you and the child. Alternatively you can make where you want to go more interesting than where the child wants to go. Why does this matter for relaxation? Your brain is like a child. It is curious and generates thoughts. That is its job just like a child's job is to explore the world. Now you can beat yourself up for your brain doing the things it is programmed to do or you can make where you are going more interesting than where your brain is trying to go.

Returning to concentration, when you heighten your concentration you increase the ability to use all of your senses so you can see, hear, smell, touch, and taste the very things you are imagining. For example, when you watch a movie you know that it is a fictional story. You know that the bad guy is just around the corner, that the heroine is heading straight for him and that it is only a matter of time before he gets her. However you also know that this is not real. This knowledge doesn't stop your body reacting as it does; that startle and jump when the bad guy jumps out. Your body reacts because your unconscious mind doesn't know the difference between what is real and what is imagined. It responds in the same way to the sensory input just to be on the safe side. This is a great device that you can take advantage of when relaxing. You can convince your body to establish that physiological state of calm and serenity by imagining a calm and serene place. You can feel your muscles unwinding, see your body relaxing, and hear the calm breath when you concentrate on your breathing in a focused and heightened way.

There are rules for relaxation

To gain the most benefit from active relaxation there are a number of things you should try to ensure happens. Try to minimize distraction by finding a quiet place, where you are less likely to be disturbed or interrupted. Let people around you know if you think it appropriate; you could even invite them to participate. I have found, as has Graham, that children can benefit from and enjoy practising these skills.

Try to do this in a room with a comfortable temperature, and use a blanket if that helps. Use a chair that supports your back. Your goal is relaxation and if you happen to fall asleep that is OK as your body does need sleep but the aim is not to sleep. Remember, relaxation here is an active process.

If you can see the benefits of relaxation for your mood, then practise early and often. Start your relaxation practice now and repeat it as often as you think about it.

Progressive muscle relaxation is an effective way to relax

This first relaxation exercise is a practical and physical technique. The outcome and skill require you to focus on your attention and heightening your concentration. The skill is being able to be relaxed when you feel as though you need it; this process is often useful when you go to bed.

It is a procedure called Progressive Muscle Relaxation. Read through this section whilst trying it, and then try it again with your eyes closed, remembering each step and noticing the changes that occur. You may want to ask someone to read this to you or alternatively record yourself saying it and play it whilst you practise the technique.

Find a comfortable chair to sit in whilst you practise. Sit comfortably on the chair, don't slouch, pay attention. Remember, relaxation is not about sleeping, it is an active practice. Start by closing your eyes while the rest of your body remains completely still. Clench your right hand tightly, now make it tighter and tighter, good, and now relax your hand completely. Notice the difference between your hand clenched tightly and what your hand feels like when it is fully relaxed. The difference between a tight muscle and a loose muscle. If you notice any feelings of warmth or heaviness when your muscle relaxes, this is your body telling you that you are on the right track. Now let your hand and arm and shoulder relax even more and as this happens your hand becomes heavier and heavier and you can't tell the difference between where your hand stops and where your leg starts. Allow your arm to slip into your lap as though you are letting go of every last bit of tension in your body.

Now clench your left hand tightly, notice it getting tighter and tighter, and then relax your hand completely. Let it go. Relax and enjoy the feeling of calm. That feeling of looseness that washes down your left arm. The warmth and heaviness that occurs as your arm becomes more and more relaxed. Again, give yourself a few moments to feel the difference between tension and relaxation – the difference between a relaxed muscle and a tense muscle.

Now bend your elbows and tense your biceps and the muscles in your upper arms. As you tense these muscles, feel the tautness like an elastic stretching, then let it go and relax your arms completely. Let your arms slide and rest again slipping down into your lap. Notice the difference as your arms lose all their tension and relax your arms completely. Let them sink heavily into your lap as the tension is washed away.

Now, forget about your hands and arms; turn your attention to your forehead. Wrinkle up your forehead as tightly as you can. Hold the tension and then relax your entire forehead and scalp. This may feel as though the muscles of your head and scalp are smooth and so relaxed they will slip off your head. Imagine your entire scalp and forehead is smooth, and relaxed. I want you now to frown; notice the strain and tension spreading across your forehead. Notice again the tension and tightness that results, and then let go. Relax your brow. Allow it to become smooth again, feel the difference between a tense and relaxed forehead. It may feel almost as if warm water is washing down your face.

Now focus on your mouth. Clench your teeth together and notice the tension throughout your jaw. Feel the tension and then relax your jaw. As your jaw relaxes your teeth will begin to part. Let your lower jaw fall loosely as all of the muscles in your scalp, forehead, face, and jaw loosen and relax. Feel the difference between the tension that was present and the relaxation you now have in your jaw. Notice how it feels for your jaw, lips, and tongue to relax fully.

Focus now on your back and shoulders. Shrug your shoulders, high up, and try to touch your ears with your shoulders. Notice the tension in your shoulders as you hunch upwards. Hold it then breathe out and relax fully. Loosen and drop your shoulders. Feel the heaviness and warmth spreading through your neck, throat, and shoulders. Full relaxation, deeper and deeper as it washes down. Feel how loose and easy your neck feels.

Now bring back your attention to take in your entire body. Give your body, your entire body a chance to relax; a chance to benefit from this great state of relaxation. Feel the comfortable and pleasant heaviness; enjoy a few breaths that flow smoothly and deeply into your abdomen. Continue to breathe slowly and deeply for a few seconds. Continue to relax. Let your breath come freely and deeply. Focus now on your stomach. Tighten your stomach muscles and hold for a few moments. Hold the tension and notice it. Then relax your stomach fully. Feel the cool air of your breath flow deeply into your lower abdomen, lifting your ribs. Feel the complete sense of relaxation as the air flows back out of your chest.

Take your attention down to your feet. Curl up your toes and clench your calves. Notice the tension for a moment or two, then relax your legs fully. Enjoy the warmth and heaviness that enters your legs as the tension flows out.

Keeping your attention with your feet, bend your foot upwards, creating tension in your shins and then relax again fully. Enjoy the heaviness that spreads throughout your legs as your muscles sink more and more heavily towards the floor, as if only the floor keeps your heavy legs from sinking downwards further. Feel the heaviness and relaxation that is present throughout your body. Enjoy the feeling of being deeply relaxed. Enjoy the sensation for a few moments.

You have now been able to notice the difference between a tense muscle and a relaxed muscle and you have done this with muscles across your entire body from the tip of your toes to the top of your head. When you are ready, open your eyes. Have a stretch and

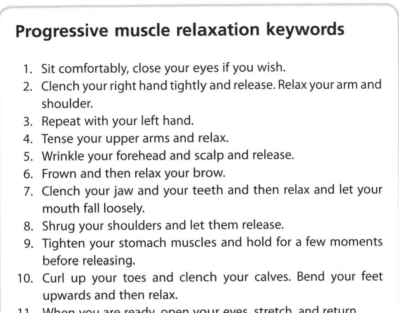

Progressive muscle relaxation keywords

1. Sit comfortably, close your eyes if you wish.
2. Clench your right hand tightly and release. Relax your arm and shoulder.
3. Repeat with your left hand.
4. Tense your upper arms and relax.
5. Wrinkle your forehead and scalp and release.
6. Frown and then relax your brow.
7. Clench your jaw and your teeth and then relax and let your mouth fall loosely.
8. Shrug your shoulders and let them release.
9. Tighten your stomach muscles and hold for a few moments before releasing.
10. Curl up your toes and clench your calves. Bend your feet upwards and then relax.
11. When you are ready, open your eyes, stretch, and return.

return your consciousness to the room, stand up and get on with your day.

You may feel this is very long-winded, but try it once slowly, and you will find it much more straightforward to do this the second time you try it. I have summarized the stages in the box above.

Don't forget to breathe!

Breathing is an automatic response to move air in and out of your lungs to take in oxygen and remove carbon dioxide from your body. The following box explains some of the associations between breathing and life expectancy. It is also a really good way to focus your concentration, and to instil relaxation. Awareness of your natural breathing forces you to concentrate on something and brings your attention to what is happening at that precise moment. It is well understood that if you can slow your breathing, then tension will reduce in your body.

Breathing and life

Breathing is one of the few bodily functions which can be controlled both consciously and unconsciously. Humans take between twelve and eighteen breaths per minute whilst they are resting. As you will be aware, exercise and stress increase the breathing rate. Some cultures and, in the past, scientists believe that each person has a total number of breaths in their lifetime. This is not particularly helpful, although there does seem to be a total number of heartbeats in a lifetime. If you are interested this has been measured at approximately one billion.

Science also knows that very physically fit athletes have slow heart rates and slow breathing. There is some evidence that breathing exercises help to maintain the quantity and quality of life.

But, it is very difficult to slow your breathing down. You may find you are artificially holding your breath, which is counterproductive. We will now introduce some breathing exercises that will allow you to focus on your breath without forcing it. Hopefully, these, given some practice, will develop concentration and calm.

To start the breathing exercise, again sit comfortably with your shoulders relaxed but paying attention. Many people find it good to close their eyes, gently. This is not essential though, and you could test out whatever feels best for you. You could do this lying down if that is more comfortable for you, or even standing up. Now think about your breathing. Mindfulness and yoga practice use breathing as a central, core, exercise for developing concentration and calm.

Try to breathe through your nose, rather than your mouth. You may breathe more naturally through your mouth, but try to use your nostrils instead to take air in and out of your lungs. Sitting with attention, breathe in through your nose, leaving your eyes shut if that is what you want to do. Feel the cool air passing over your nostrils and into your lungs. Then exhale, again feeling warmed air pass out of your nose. How does that feel? Do this for a few breaths. Now count whilst taking an in-breath, again always through your nose if you can. Try now, on the next exhale, to breathe out for the same number of counts as when you breathed in. Many people find that they can breathe in through their nostrils quicker and with less force than breathing out.

The intention here is to regulate the pace of your breathing, which may require some conscious effort, but try not to force a breath. Allow yourself to breathe normally, whilst continuously focusing on your breathing.

You may have counted to four, or five, or many more, on your in-breath. This is not a competition, so whatever number you counted to is fine. See whether, as you are doing this, you count to a larger number after a few breaths. When you have finished, open your eyes and take a large stretch. You are now ready to return to your life again.

You could use this exercise in many different situations. You could do this on a train, or in your chair at work. It takes just a few minutes, but can provide real focus. It can be a particularly helpful exercise to do before a stressful situation, to ground yourself and your thoughts. In the same way as for progressive muscle relaxation, the box below has a summary of the key stages.

Breathing consciously

1. Sit comfortably, shoulders relaxed, paying attention. Close your eyes, gently.
2. Breathe through your nostrils, keeping your eyes shut.
3. Count for the time it takes to breathe in.
4. Count whilst exhaling for the same number as it took for the in-breath.
5. Breathe normally, whilst continuously focusing on your breathing.
6. Open your eyes, stretch your arms, and return to the room.

Other breathing exercises

These next exercises help to slow down your breathing by focusing your attention and heightening your concentration. If you breathe quickly, then you are taking very shallow breaths from the top half of your chest. When you pant you are taking quick shallow breaths. When you are relaxed, your breath comes from the diaphragm, opens your chest and slows down your breathing. The balloon belly exercise can demonstrate how to breathe slowly, from the diaphragm.

Sit up straight in your chair and place your hands flat upon the area just above your belly button just below your chest. Move your hands so that your fingertips are just touching each other and make sure your hands are resting gently. Now take deep slow breaths as if you were breathing out of your belly button. This sounds strange but focus on your belly button. You will know if you are breathing deeply because your fingertips will move slightly apart from one another as you breathe in. Hold onto the bit at the end of each out-breath, that relaxed, calm feeling.

Practise this until you are breathing slowly and deeply with your fingertips moving gently away from one another then back to touching, each time you breathe in and out.

Another technique is one used by people who pursue the practice of yoga nidra or yogic sleep. This is a practice gaining popularity and has a particular breathing technique that I will describe here. This one may be best practised whilst lying flat on a comfortable surface – but not a bed, which should only be used for sleeping! Try to find a good place to lie that you do not associate with sleeping. Obviously if you are using this technique to help you fall asleep lying on the bed is appropriate.

Lie comfortably, place your hands at the side of your body with the palms of your hand facing upwards towards the ceiling or sky. This is known in yoga as shavasana, or rather disturbingly the corpse pose. Focus on breathing through your nose, and then take an in- and out-breath. Say eleven in your mind, then take another gentle, relaxing, breath and say to yourself ten. Continue counting backwards, from eleven to one. For a deeper relaxation start at twenty-seven and count back to one. To maintain the sensation, once you reach the number one in the countdown, you can continue breathing, repeating the number one as a focus. This focus also helps to dismiss intruding thoughts.

Mindfulness is not about emptying your mind

The techniques described will require your attention and work, but are only starting to develop your practice of relaxation. There is a growing reputation for using a technique known as mind-fulness for controlling mood. Mindfulness can be most simply defined as knowing what is happening when it is happening, no matter what is happening. Mindfulness is both a process of striving to achieve this and the outcome when you achieve this state.

The practice involves paying attention, to the moment you are experiencing, in a non-judgemental manner. This includes atten-tion to a number of different domains, both to sounds, what you see, how your body feels physically, what emotions you are feeling, and the thoughts in your mind. Traditionally a Buddhist practice, it has a focus on being healthy and removing the habits and filters that cause our mind to ruminate and not challenge unhelpful thinking styles and eventually limit our options for life. These limi-tations occur by not living in the moment.

As a result of mindfulness practice, your relationship with your experience will change. The way you think, how you feel, and the sensations and urges you have are important and mindfulness lets you experience them in a different way. Your thoughts become a process where your mind is focusing your attention on a particular thought at that particular time. A wholesome relationship is often the result, seeing yourself as a person and more than just your thoughts, an experience, or outcome. Mindfulness results in you seeing yourself as a person who recognizes that change is constant.

There are several important components here. Firstly, your atten-tion is focused and not slipping back into the past and how things should have been different or other fantasies about alternate pasts: "if only this had happened then I would be better off as this bad thing would not have occurred". Equally, when you are mindful, your attention stays in the present and is not concerned with the creation of an alternate future. These "if only . . . then . . ." state-ments are disarmed by mindfulness.

Mindfulness has a lot to do with the skills of attention. By focusing your attention you can enjoy the benefit of your awareness as it becomes richer. With practice, the mindful experience becomes more non-judgemental. This frees you from the thoughts of having to do something in order to change things. I once saw a bumper sticker and it said "Meditation . . . , it is better than sitting there doing nothing". Humans are prone to want to change, alter, adapt, and modify their environment. Mindfulness is about rest, different to the focus of much of modern day society.

First practice mindfulness with your toothbrush

There are many ways to develop mindful practice. A good starting point is to incorporate this sort of approach to everyday activities. How about, the next time you brush your teeth, which is normally a mindless experience, try to adopt some mindfulness. As you pick up your toothbrush, how does it feel, what is its temperature, is it wet or dry? As you put toothpaste onto your brush, what noise does it make? How does it look, what is the colour, the texture?

As you then start to clean your teeth, try to be engulfed by the experience, focus on the tastes, the temperatures, the feelings you have. Think only about that experience, do not give thought to anything else.

If a thought comes into your mind, which it will, try to label it "thought" and bring your attention back to the activity. Return to the experience with your toothbrush and cleaning your teeth. This may seem an odd thing to do, but it is a glimpse of the world of mindfulness, where you focus on your feelings, things happening in your day, and external events. You have, hopefully, gently discarded the thinking.

The amazing thing about the human brain is that it constantly jumps from one thought to the next. This is what everyone does, but this means you cannot rest your mind. You have rested your body earlier in this chapter, but this will allow you to rest your mind. This can be really difficult, and you will catch yourself thinking of something again, that leads to more thoughts. It's not easy and will require practice, with the intention of being able to rest your mind for short periods of time.

Mindfulness helps people to develop strategies and skills for dealing with emotions and thoughts that are not helpful. But, in the first instance, mindfulness may also give short-term strategies for getting through difficult situations.

You could try this with many other everyday activities, such as when you take a shower, or take a walk to work or the bus stop.

Try to extend mindfulness – bit by bit

When you are comfortable with a routinely done activity and applying some mindfulness, then why not try to spend two minutes on this when you wake? This has been found to be a good time to set the tone for the day. On waking, be mindful of what is happening – noises, the light, warmth, how the bed feels on your body.

Take a scan through your body. Start in your toes and try to think how they are feeling. Then scan up your body, your lower legs, knees, upper legs. How your buttocks and groin feel, your stomach and chest. Are there any pains or discomfort in your back? Work through your fingers, hands, arms to your shoulders. Then think about your head, scalp, eyes, nose, mouth. This scan is a good way to start your day and prepare for whatever is going to come your way.

Short bursts of mindfulness may feel easy to do, and therefore you may think they won't be of much use, but I find short bursts are very effective. Many daily practitioners of this use no more than 20 minutes per day as a good length of time to focus their mind and begin their day.

"Post-it" note technique

As you practise relaxation and mindfulness, you will notice that you become more aware of when your body is tense and not relaxed. When you don't feel relaxed, your shoulders may feel tense and raised up towards your ears. If this is the case, then simply by relaxing your shoulders you will feel calmer.

To demonstrate another example, Graham, when he has some serious tension before speaking to large groups of people, has a feeling that his heart will burst open from his chest. Graham has found that focusing on his breathing will allow a feeling of calm to appear.

On a "post-it" note, write down the signs that you notice in your body when you do not feel relaxed. You may find this difficult to begin with, but as you practise relaxation techniques, these signs will become more apparent.

For those of you who find this practice useful, you could consider extending it to meditation. This is the next step in mindfulness. There are many different versions of meditation, and you may need to try out different sorts before you find one right for you. Meditation at the start will be most productive with guided practice. This may be a pre-recorded session that you buy, or having a guide in person. These methods work well for most people, and take this experience up a level.

Seeing things as they are helps you to establish insight

Mindfulness helps you to take responsibility for the experiences you have, be they thoughts, feelings or sensations. Of importance is knowing that you as a person do not need to be defended, approved of, compared to objects of status, or to justify your actions.

When I talk about this process I am talking about insight, or the capacity to gain an accurate and intuitive understanding of yourself. You may have picked up this book because you have insight that the symptoms you are experiencing are due to something going amiss. When you recognize that your problems are getting in the way of work or that your thoughts and actions are unreasonable, but you do it anyway, this is an example of insight. Other people with eating disorders, Alzheimer's disease, or schizophrenia are often less likely to see they have anything wrong in their lives or that their symptoms are getting in the way.

Rogers identified ". . . that the process of achieving insight is likely to involve more adequate facing of reality as it exists within the self, as well as external reality; that it involves the relating of problems to each other, the perception of patterns of behaviour; that it involves the acceptance of hitherto denied elements of the self, and a reformulating of the self-concept; and that it involves the making of new plans."

The insight can be shallow or complex, involving the view taken on a series of events or bringing forth a new personality. In Client Centred Therapy (CCT), the clinician trusts the patient to provide the insights, direct the therapy, and within a trusted therapy environment, this happens. The parallels with mindfulness are strong. Mindfulness practice trusts you to guide the process, see the insights as they arise, and develop the best place for this to take root. Time is an important aspect here. In therapy, just as in mindfulness practice, there is no place you need to go, nothing you need to do. Just breathe in the here and now. In CCT, the therapist trusts in the integrative, spontaneous nature of the client and in mindfulness you are practising integrating your experience, allowing spontaneity to enter your life and enabling this to become more of your life, by practice.

When you heighten your concentration you are able to notice more of life that is going on around you. This characteristic means you can allow the experiences that you have in everyday life to be like water off a duck's back. By controlling your attention you can increase your awareness of when feelings or thoughts become the single determining factor in your experience. Like a picture on a piece of paper, when you hold the picture close to your face, then the image takes up your entire view, giving you a false belief that the picture is all there is to see. But as you control your view, you can hold the picture at arm's length and know that the picture is but one part of your experience. Also, you are in control of how close or indeed how far away you hold that image.

My grandfather would often give me advice to stop and smell the roses. What does this mean exactly? The idea again is to focus your attention and heighten your concentration. Concentrate on what data comes through your senses; what do you see, hear, smell, touch, and taste? How do other people describe similar situations?

We have discussed the importance of naming feelings in this book as a way of helping manage your moods. Try this when you are practising mindfulness and move beyond just feelings into thoughts, sensations, and what you are doing. Try describing the thought you just had, for example "I had a thought about the next bill I have to pay". Your thoughts or any other aspect of your experience is not your whole experience. You are made up of your experiences, personality, thoughts, and so much more. A thought is simply one outcome of your brain generating your mind which creates a thought about what you are focusing your attention on right now. Try saying the above sentence again but slowly to yourself: "A thought is simply one outcome of my brain generating my mind which creates a thought about what I am focusing my attention on right now."

The links with mindfulness, as an analysis of past experience with the purpose of gaining insight, is attractive. Simulations of future possible scenarios might be seen as useful to try and predict outcomes. However, as we have seen in practice and research when insight is not held to account by a method such as the "scientific method", errors in thinking can result. That is, did your predictions *really* match what ended up happening?

One aspect of mindfulness that is critical here is a non-judgemental stance. By describing just the facts you remove the likelihood of your mood influencing your perspective. By focusing on the "what, when, where, how and who" you decrease the chance of bias coming into your thinking. Those four-letter words like nice, must, and fine described in Chapter 6 "Unhappiness", are important here.

Mindfulness means there is no good or must or fine. There is and there is not. Now as I have mentioned, the propensity for you to engage in bias and be influenced by your mood is very much part of the human condition. Given that you recognize this, when you find yourself judging yourself, remember to not judge your judging.

With regular practice these techniques will bring rewards

This chapter has taken you through several relaxation techniques, how relaxation techniques influence your mood, and how practising these techniques can help in managing mood problems. Your

"Post-it" note technique

As we have seen above, there are many ways you can introduce relaxation into your everyday life. Mindfulness involves practice. Focusing on some object for five minutes at a time helps us to increase our ability to focus, calms the mind, and allows the body to relax. Sit quietly each day and relax your mind by breathing deeply. Write down the time on a "post-it" note and just watch your breath, aware of when you inhale and exhale. As your awareness increases, your breathing will become steady and you will be able to feel relaxed and focused. Write down the time you stop on that same "post-it" note. Stick the notes on your wall, one for each day for two weeks.

mind will behave like a child does in the world, in a curious and playful manner. Our aim was to draw your focus onto the more desirable destination of relaxation, rather than on all the distracting curiosities on the way. You can become aware of the distractions and label them. This allows you to experiment with your experience, thoughts, and feelings by watching them float by. Using your five senses, and using them more fully, allows both an enjoyment of the journey and the destination. With practice and the rewards it can bring, relaxation can provide freedom and control of your mood.

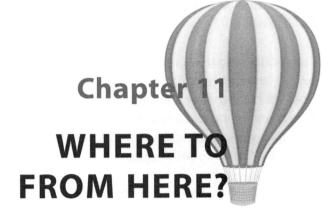

Chapter 11

WHERE TO FROM HERE?

"*Don't take this the wrong way, but I hope I don't see you again!*"

This is something that patients often say to me at the end of their therapy, and similarly, now that we have come to the end of the book, we hope that you are now in a much stronger position to make changes and feel good. We started the book with hope, your hope that you could make changes and feel good. Similarly we aim to end the book with hope.

It would be awfully blunt to say the sky is falling in and that if you don't change your ways then we are all doomed. I can show how research demonstrates the increasingly "individualistic" values in western society, the rising rate of mental illness, and how materialism is a driving force bringing our culture to the brink. Instead, we have spoken about inter-connectedness, diversity, equality, living a conscious and self-aware life. By the end of this book you will realize that you have a set of skills to help prevent your mood causing problems, assess your strengths, and look forward to the challenges ahead.

It is important to assess the progress that you have made

Every six to ten sessions I measure a patient's progress. The aim in that session is to work out how they were when they started therapy, get a better understanding of how far they have come, and answer the important question: Where to from here?

Think back to how life was for you when you picked up this book and started reading it. If you remember, the first "post-it" note technique asked just this question; why did you buy this book? I asked you to keep it somewhere safe and now is the time to look back at it and remember how you felt when you wrote it. If you are unable to find it don't worry – we are all only human! I would be surprised if you aren't a little shocked as you recognize how far you have come in the last few weeks. I wonder whether anyone else has commented on the changes you have made. Simply the fact that someone notices is a common motivator that encourages further change.

A useful technique is to think back to a situation that went badly for you in the past. This may be an argument with a friend, a time that you felt anxious and therefore avoided doing something, or a hurtful comment made about you by someone else. Try to replay the situation in your mind or write it down and think about how you would handle it now with the new skills you have learnt. This process provides an understanding of how much progress you have made, the challenges you have overcome in battling your mood issues, and the strengths you have uncovered.

My goal is to equip you with the skills to be your own therapist; to recognize where problems are occurring, to self-manage these issues while integrating and improving in the areas you identify. Your goal is improvement not perfection.

You will need to "let go" of old habits

Often the road to progress is about letting go. This is a practised skill, not a warm feeling accompanied by classical music playing in the background and a fuzzy filter on the camera lens of life. The process of "letting go" can be a physical change in the things you do, a shift in your thinking; a letting go of the beliefs and feelings you are maintaining that hold you back and you fear living without. In Chapter 2 "Challenge your thinking", I spoke about the system of beliefs that are restrictive, inaccurate, and unrealistic. You have practised techniques that help let go of these behaviours, thoughts, and feelings.

Reviewing your progress provides an excellent opportunity to let go and understand that you are not your past. Try to think of this letting go as a little like reading an obituary of a person you are glad is not around anymore. You will find you get better when you stop ruminating on why and simply let go. Why you did something in the past or indeed didn't do something in the past. Why you don't initiate change to improve your life now or why things external to you don't change to make your life a better place. Focus on the what, when, where, how, and who; rather than on the why. This isn't an attempt to avoid this question but it often remains something outside of your grasp. Therefore this is a recognition that you need to work on what you can change.

Monitoring progress will help you to prevent relapse

Preventing relapse and recurrence is acknowledging the role you play in decreasing the risk of mood problems. Scheduling a mood check-up and online mood measures are good for this, allowing you to review your emotions and the ways you have to cope with each of them.

Knowing the risk factors to slipping back or relapsing is often useful as you are in a position to prevent further deterioration. To go for a period of time without symptoms is a great achievement and not undone by the recurrence of a mood problem. The risk factors associated with relapse and recurrence of mood problems often have roots in the past. The number and severity of previous mood problems, a shorter time being well, stress, and limited social support all are important. Having worked through this book is an achievement in itself and should have equipped you with the knowledge to recognize when problems are developing at an earlier stage, so that you can effectively tackle them without letting things spiral out of control.

This allows you to grow in terms of your insight, humour, creativity, and openness. You are building the capacity to move from seeing parts of your experience as high risk to something that is a great challenge. You have taken risks in applying some of the techniques used in the book, decreasing your likelihood of avoidance and challenging yourself in new ways.

Once progress has been made it needs to be maintained

Prevention is often about seeing the areas of grey between the categories we draw arbitrarily. It involves testing the requirement for worry, assessing the risks involved and the impact if this thing were to happen. It is a focus on the here and now, not the past or the future.

SWOT analysis is a planning method whereby the Strengths, Weaknesses or limitations, Opportunities, and Threats involved in attaining a goal are listed. This method can be used to specify the goals that you want to achieve and identify the internal and external resources associated with the attainment of this goal, as well as the risks involved. This process can help to clearly develop the steps you require on your road ahead.

The strengths remind you to do the work required. By practising the "post-it" note techniques you will hopefully have had the self-motivation required to keep working through the book. What strengths have you attained whilst doing this?

The weaknesses or limitations identified at this time are the internal problems that make attainment of the goal difficult. Rumination and the negative statements you make about yourself are often the greatest challenge. Cynicism, self-doubt, and self-criticism may be well worn tracks, embedded over many years. Hopefully in the same way that you have developed many strengths whilst reading this book you have also developed skills to overcome these problems. Realistic problem solving is often a new skill and, when you first apply this, can seem difficult to integrate and use well.

It is very much like when you first start to drive a car. When I first started driving, I had to have the radio off, the windows up in order to listen closely to the engine, and no one could speak as it would put me off my driving. My driving was a very deliberate act and felt strange and foreign to me. Now I drive with music playing, listening to my daughter sing, and I might even sing myself. Problem-solving thinking can become an equally embedded and automatic habit leaving you free from the doubt associated with learning new experiences.

When I think of opportunity, the wise words of Churchill come to mind "A pessimist sees the difficulty in every opportunity; an optimist sees the opportunity in every difficulty." Perception is the key here. It is important to keep this in mind when difficulties come along as they inevitably will do. If you can see them as an opportunity to practise the skills you have worked on you will find they present less of a problem.

What are the threats that have been effective triggers for your mood to suffer in the past? Accepting that you may experience problems again at some time, what kind of things are likely to set you back? How could you deal with them? Who is there at home who could help you if necessary?

"Post-it" note technique

It can be very beneficial to make a note of your strengths and opportunities. Take a "post-it" note and list your strengths. Sometimes these strengths can only be seen by an objective outsider and it is helpful to take note when someone comments on a strength you have acquired. I remember a colleague once commenting that I remained calm at work whatever challenges were presented. I remember this conversation when dealing with a difficult or stressful situation. What other strengths do you have?

Then take a second "post-it" note and list the opportunities that you have. These can be big or small. Can you watch that new movie, or read that classic novel you always wanted to read? Or something big like thinking about a career change. Anything is an opportunity. The goal here is not necessarily to take these opportunities, but to realize what you would have to do if you wanted to.

Recognizing need is what keeps me going

Ask yourself the following questions:

- What evidence is there that this book has worked or been helpful for you?
- What have you learned?
- How can you build on what you have learned so as to make yourself as independent and confident as possible?

Please grant me an opportunity to indulge in talking about myself. What keeps a psychologist going in my opinion is the ongoing training, supervision, and nature of the work itself. I do work that is meaningful to me and in an environment that allows some creativity and independence. Every day I get to hear other people's stories and importantly tell my own in a way that supports them. Sharing my experiences is an essential way to build rapport, offer different perspectives, and let others know that I am human, with all the strengths and frailties that that involves. Listening to you describe the depth of your experience provides me an opportunity to highlight key points. When I tell people what I do, they often focus their attention on the positive impact I must be making. This is important and motivating but not the whole story and definitely not the reason I became a psychologist.

When I first started my working life as a psychologist, I was driven by the overwhelming needs of others. Abuse, despair, and terminal illness were the pools I immersed myself in, being a life saver and boldly heading for the seashore. Since I was cynical and felt stripped of the privileges of others around me, it was easy to find areas of despair and, with my familiarity with them, appear confident swimming alongside others who happened to be my patients at the time. The more I immersed myself, the more deeply I saw the need and the more self-righteous I became; on the surface presenting a cool aloofness and beneath kicking harder and harder against the tide and sometimes the very person I was trying to save. At these times, I didn't accept the person's experience as valid but more as a view that needed correcting. I was failing to see myself for who I was and others as who they were. Both of us are quite able to float and with strengths of our own.

Often those in the helping profession see those in need and it is the actual need we focus on. I accept that the person is in need and I take the perspective of a change agent, where I attempt

"Post-it" note technique

On a "post-it" note, write down the answers to the following questions about yourself: What has changed the most for you? What are the most important things at this time in your life? What are you most afraid of in your life? What are you doing about it?

to shift you from the observer of life to the actor. This only occurs once I have your understanding, trust, and confidence. My successful time with patients is when they leave me and then do something and often that something is shifting their perspective and allowing me the privilege of being with them in that journey back to the shore. Often you can't make this journey on your own but you too are doing the same thing as I am in each session. It is the focus on your own needs and the needs of others that keeps you and indeed me going.

Final "post-it" note technique

You have worked through the book. It is now time to evaluate how you have changed, how you have improved, what has happened to your mood. Look again at that "post-it" note from Chapter 1 "How are you?"

Take a look at what you hoped to achieve, to improve, what your goals were. How does this match with what you have done? What success you have had? You also rated your confidence in achieving this. How does this match with how you now feel?

Now take a new "post-it" note. Again write down on this what your goals are now. What things do you want to improve further in your life? Store this somewhere safe, and return to this periodically to explore how you are getting on. That is how we will leave you, with this gift from yourself.

AFTERWORD

Thank you for being on this journey with us. As we described in the Preface, writing this book has been an important goal for our lives. As a psychologist, I intended to pass on some of the wisdom I have gained in my years of practice. All of the people I have seen in my professional and personal life have also contributed to this and I thank them for that. Graham has enjoyed bringing his understanding of the world of science and his experience of the techniques for relaxation to this.

When I see a person in my practice, at the end of each session I ask a simple question "How did this session go for you?" To help with this, I provide a rating scale to fill in, on scales such as acceptance, hope, honesty, helpfulness and ask them to circle the number that best describes their reaction.

We would feel privileged to have your feedback on how you feel this session has gone, through email (pascoepsychology@gmail.com).

Using the scale in the box on the next page, write down your ratings after reading this book. Using a scale to rate your feelings can be useful to create a snapshot of your mood and also to open up other questions about your progress using the techniques provided in this book. By rating your progress with your goals generally, we can identify the strengths you have used. Also, by rating where you are now, the road ahead will seem more clear. Questions like what will you be doing differently if you are at a 7 instead of a 6? What is the smallest thing you can do today to move just 0.5 points along the scale? Please be honest as the information will only be useful if you show what you genuinely think and feel about the session.

Final assessment

Helpfulness										
0	1	2	3	4	5	6	7	8	9	10
The book was not helpful				Neutral			I found the book helpful			
Hope										
0	1	2	3	4	5	6	7	8	9	10
I felt hopeless after reading the book				Neutral			I felt hopeful after reading the book			
Understanding of myself										
0	1	2	3	4	5	6	7	8	9	10
I didn't get any new understanding about myself from this book				Neutral			I have a better understanding of myself as a result of this			
How confident are you about achieving those goals?										
0	1	2	3	4	5	6	7	8	9	10
I'm not at all confident				Neutral			I am very confident			
Goals										
0	1	2	3	4	5	6	7	8	9	10
I am not at all close to achieving my goals				Neutral			I have achieved the goals I came here for			

BIBLIOGRAPHY AND FURTHER READING

Chapter 1

Mercier, H. and Sperber, D. (2011) Why do Humans Reason? Arguments for an argumentative theory. *Behavioural and Brain Sciences* 34: 57–74.

Parsons, T. (1951) *The Social System*. Glencoe, IL: The Free Press.

Chapter 2

Bechara, A., Damasio, H., Tranel, D., and Damasio, A.R. (1997) Deciding Advantageously Before Knowing the Advantageous Strategy. *Science* 28: 5304.

Ditto, P.H. and Lopez, D.F. (1992) Motivated Scepticism: Use of differential decision criteria for preferred and nonpreferred conclusions. *Journal of Personality and Social Psychology* 63: 568–84.

Eagleman, D. (2011) *Incognito: The Secret Lives of the Brain*. Melbourne: Penguin Australia.

Floris Cohen, H. (1994) Letter to J.S. Switzer (23 April 1953), quoted in *The Scientific Revolution: A Historiographical Inquiry*, p. 234.

Gladwell, M. (2007) *Blink: The Power of Thinking Without Thinking*. London: Penguin.

Heatherton, T.F. and Nichols, P.A. (1994) Personal Accounts of Successful versus Failed Attempts at Life Change. *Personality and Social Psychology Bulletin* 20: 664–75.

Hobbes, T. (1651, 2010) *Leviathan: Or the Matter, Forme, and Power of a Common-Wealth Ecclesiasticall and Civill*, ed. by Ian Shapiro. Yale: University Press.

Hsee, C.K. and Hastie, R. (2006) Decision and Experience: Why don't we choose what makes us happy? *Trends in Cognitive Sciences* 10: 31–7.

Jones, E.E. and Harris, V.A. (1967) The Attribution of Attitudes. *Journal of Experimental Social Psychology* 3: 1–24.

Kahneman, D. (2011) *Thinking Fast and Slow*. London: Penguin.

Koestler, A. (1971) *The Act of Creation*. London: Pan Piper.

Llewellyn, J. (2007) In a Confusing Climate. *The Observer*, 2 September.

Lord, C., Ross, L., and Lepper, M. (1979) Biased Assimilation and Attitude Polarization: The effects of prior theories on subsequently considered evidence. *Journal of Personality and Social Psychology* 37: 2098–109.

Mercier, H. and Sperber, D. (2009) Intuitive and Reflective Inferences. In J.St.B.T. Evans and K. Frankish, *Two Minds: Dual Processes and Beyond*. Oxford: Oxford University Press.

Mercier, H. and Sperber, D. (2011) Why do Humans Reason? Arguments for an argumentative theory. *Behavioural and Brain Sciences* 34: 57–74.

Moore, M.T. and Fresco, D. (2007) Depressive Realism and Attributional Style: Implications for individuals at risk for depression. *Behavior Therapy* 38: 144–54.

Okada, E.M. (2005) Justification Effects on Consumer Choice of Hedonic and Utilitarian Goods. *Journal of Marketing Research* 42: 43–53.

Sackett, D.L., Rosenberg, W.M., Gray, J.A., Haynes, R.B., and Richardson, W.S. (1996) Evidence Based Medicine: What it is and what it isn't. *British Medical Journal* 312: 71–2.

Scioli, A., Chamberlin, C.M., Samor, C.M., Lapointe, A.B., Campbell, T.L., MacLeod, A.R., and McLenon, J. (1997) A Prospective Study of Hope, Optimism, and Health. *Psychological Reports* 81: 723–33.

Thayer, V.T. (1922) *A Comparison of the Ethical Philosophics of Spinoza and Hobbes*. Library of Congress Archives.

Tversky, A. and Kahneman, D. (1974) Judgment under Uncertainty: Heuristics and Biases. *Science* 185: 1124–31.

Tversky, A., Sattath, S., and Slovic, P. (1988) Contingent Weighting in Judgment and Choice. *Psychological Review* 95: 371–84.

Vroling, M.S. and de Jong, P.J. (2009) Deductive Reasoning and Social Anxiety: Evidence for a fear-confirming belief bias. *Cognitive Therapy Research* 33: 633–44.

Chapter 3

Adler, A. (1959) *The Practice and Theory of Individual Psychology.* Totowa, NJ: Littlefield Adams.

Corney, R.H. (1990) A Survey of Professional Help Sought by Patients for Psychosocial Problems. *British Journal of General Practice* 40: 365–8.

Mahon, N.E., Yarcheski, A., Yarcheski, T.J., and Hanks, M.M. (2010) A Meta-analytic Study of Predictors of Anger in Adolescents. *Nursing Research* 59: 178–84.

Monte, C.F. (1995) *Beneath the Mask: An introduction to theories of personality.* Orlando, FL: Harcourt Brace College Publishers.

Schopenhauer, A. (1851) *Studies in Pessimism.* http://ebooks. adelaide.edu.au/s/schopenhauer/arthur/pessimism/index.html.

Tudiver, F. and Talbot, Y. (1999) Why Don't Men Seek Help? Family physicians' perspectives on help-seeking behavior in men. *Journal of Family Practice* 48: 47–52.

Chapter 4

Ashford, S., Edmunds, J., and French, D.P. (2010) What is the Best Way to Change Self-efficacy to Promote Lifestyle and Recreational Physical Activity? A systematic review with meta-analysis. *British Journal of Health Psychology* 15: 265–88.

Bandura, A. (1977) Self-efficacy: Toward a unifying theory of behavioral change. *Psychological Review* 84: 191–215.

Bandura, A. (1994) Self-efficacy. In Ramachaudran V.S. (ed.) *Encyclopedia of Human Behavior* (Vol. 4, pp. 71–81). New York: Academic Press. (Reprinted in H. Friedman [ed.], *Encyclopedia of Mental Health*. San Diego: Academic Press, 1998).

Bandura, A. and Locke, E.A. (2003) Negative Self-efficacy and Goal Effects revisited. *Journal of Applied Psychology* 88: 87–99.

Judge, T.A. and Bono, J.E. (2001) Relationship of Core Self-evaluation Traits – Self-esteem, generalized self-efficacy, locus of control, and emotional stability – with job satisfaction and job performance: A meta-analysis. *Journal of Applied Psychology* 86: 80–92.

Seligman, M.E., Rashid, T., and Parks, A.C. (2006) Positive Psychotherapy. *American Psychologist* 61: 774–88.

Chapter 5

Coon, D. and Mitterer, J.O. (2007) *Introduction to psychology.* Belmont, CA: Thomson Wadsworth.

Cox, T. and McKay, C. (1978) Stress at Work. In T. Cox (ed.) *Stress.* Baltimore: University Park Press.

DuPont, R.L., DuPont Spencer, E., and DuPont, C.M. (2003) *The Anxiety Cure: An Eight-Step Program for Getting Well.* Hoboken, NJ: John Wiley & Sons.

Newhart, Bob (2001) extract from 'Stop it!' sketch on MADtv.

Chapter 6

Koestler, A. (1971) *The Act of Creation.* London: Pan Piper.

Reanney, D. (1994) *Music of the Mind: An adventure into consciousness.* Melbourne: Hill of Content Publishing Company.

Shavitt, S., Sanbonmatsu, D.M., Smittipatana, S., and Posavac, S.S. (1999) Broadening the Conditions for Illusory Correlation Formation: Implications for judging minority groups. *Basic and Applied Social Psychology* 21: 263–79.

Sweeney, P.D., Anderson, K., and Bailey, S. (1986) Attributional Style in Depression: A meta-analytic review. *Journal of Personality and Social Psychology* 50: 974–91.

Chapter 7

Bircher, J. (2005) Towards a Dynamic Definition of Health and Disease. *Medical Health Care Philosophy* 8: 335–41.

Bloom, P. (2010) *How Pleasure Works: The new science of why we like what we like.* New York: Norton.

Chibnall, J.T., Videen, S.D., Duckro, P.N., and Miller, D.K. (2002) Psychosocial-Spiritual Correlates of Death Distress in Patients with Life-threatening Medical Conditions. *Palliative Medicine* 16: 331–8.

Emmons, R. (2007) *Thanks!: How the New Science of Gratitude Can Make You Good*. New York: Houghton Mifflin Harcourt.

Gilbert, D. (2007) *Stumbling on Happiness*. New York: First Vantage Books.

Hann, D.M., Oxman, T.E., Ahles, T.A., Furstenberg, C.T. and Stuke, T.A. (1995) Social Support Adequacy and Depression in Older Patients with Metastatic Cancer. *Psycho-Oncology* 4: 213–21.

Heatherton, T.F. and Nichols, P.A. (1994) Personal Accounts of Successful versus Failed Attempts at Life Change. *Personality and Social Psychology Bulletin* 20: 664–75.

James, W. (1890) *The Principles of Psychology*. New York: Holt.

Kornblith, A.B. (1998) Psychosocial Adaptation of Cancer Survivors. In J.H.R. McKorkle (ed.) *Psycho-oncology*. Oxford: Oxford University Press, pp. 223–41.

Murchison, C. (1930) *Autobiography of Robert Mearns Yerkes*. Worcester: Clark University Press.

Seligman, M.E.P. (2012). *Flourish: A Visionary New Understanding of Happiness and Well-being*. New York: Free Press.

WHO (1946) Preamble to the Constitution of the World Health Organization as adopted by the International Health Conference, New York.

Wood, A.M., Froh, J.J., Geraghty, A.W.A. (2010) Gratitude and Well-being: A review and theoretical integration. *Clinical Psychology Review* 30: 890–905.

Wortman, C.B. (1984) Social Support and the Cancer Patient: Conceptual and Methodologic issues. *Cancer* 53: 2339–62.

Chapter 8

Blackhart, G.C., Nelson, B.C., Knowles, M.L., and Baumeister, R.F. (2009) Rejection Elicits Emotional Reactions but Neither Causes Immediate Distress nor Lowers Self-esteem: A meta-analytic review of 192 studies on social exclusion. *Personality and Social Psychology Review* 13: 269–309.

Branden, N. (2004) *The Six Pillars of Self-Esteem*. New York: Bantam Books.

Crowley, M. (2001) Empowerment: Helping vulnerable individuals enhance their degree of controls. *Psychotherapy in Australia* 7(2 Feb): 12–7.

Deci, E.L. and Ryan, R.M. (1995) Human Autonomy: The basis for true self-esteem. In M. Kernis (ed.) *Efficacy, agency, and self-esteem*. New York: Plenum Publishing Co., pp. 31–49.

VanDellen, M., Knowles, M.L., Krusemark, E., Sabet, R.F., Campbell, W.K., McDowell, J.E., and Clementz, B.A. (2012) Trait Self-esteem Moderates Decreases in Self-control Following Rejection: An Information-processing Account. *European Journal of Personality* 26: 123–32.

Chapter 9

Field, T., Diego, M., Delgado, J., and Medina, L. (2013) Tai Chi/Yoga Reduces Prenatal Depression, Anxiety and Sleep Disturbances. *Complementary Therapy and Clinical Practice* 19: 6–10.

Kaplan, J. (ed) (2002) *Bartlett's Familiar Quotations*, 17th Ed. New York: Little, Brown & Company, p735.

Kivetz, R., Urminsky, O., and Zheng, Y. (2006) The Goal-Gradient Hypothesis Resurrected: Purchase Acceleration, Illusionary Goal Progress, and Customer Retention. *Journal of Marketing Research* 43: 39–58.

Miller, W.R. (1993) What I Would Most Like to Know: What really drives change? *Addiction* 88: 1479–80.

Moliver, N., Mika, E.M., Chartrand, M.S., Haussmann, R. and Khalsa, S. (2013) Yoga Experience as a Predictor of Psychological Wellness in Women over 45 Years. *International Journal of Yoga* 6: 11–19.

Skinner, N., Hutchinson, C., and Pocock, B. (2012) *The Big Squeeze: Work, Life and Care in 2012 – The Australian Work and Life Index*. Centre for Work and Life, University of SA.

Chapter 10

Rogers, C.R. (1984) *A therapists view of psychotherapy*. Trowbridge, Wiltshire: Redwood Burns Limited.

INDEX